TIMELESS
VIRTUES

TIMELESS VIRTUES

LESSONS
IN CHARACTER
FOR WOMEN

Dellanna W. O'Brien

New Hope Publishers
Birmingham, Alabama

New Hope Publishers
P. O. Box 12065
Birmingham, AL 35202-2065
www.newhopepubl.com

Library of Congress Cataloging-in-Publication Data

O'Brien, Dellanna.
  Timeless virtues : lessons in character for women / Dellanna W. O'Brien.
      p. cm.
  ISBN 1-56309-727-3 (softcover)
  1. Christian women—Religious life. 2. Virtues. I. Title.
  BV4527 .O37 2002
  248.8'43—dc21
                                        2001007009

Cover design by Cheryl Totty

ISBN: 1-56309-727-3
N014115 • 0402 • 5M1

To my husband, Bill O'Brien,
who for almost fifty years
has been my wisest teacher,
greatest cheerleader
and best friend.

Contents

What do the words noble, virtuous, capable, and truly good have in common? They are all descriptions in Proverbs 31:10–31 of the ideal woman in Old Testament times. She rises at dawn while it is dark to begin her busy day as cook and cleaner, weaver and seamstress, international trader, physical laborer, gardener, entrepreneur, teacher, wife, and mother—managing all the while to dress elegantly, keep a good sense of humor and "laugh at the time to come."

My husband simply hums "The Impossible Dream" at this list, but Joan, a friend of mine, wants to know where the female servants mentioned in verse 15 are. I have been through my address book listing all my friends and have thumbed through an encyclopedia listing famous women of all time, and I have failed to find anyone who satisfies all the characteristics in this passage. If one could find such a superwoman, where is the perfect man to claim this prize?

Actually, most theologians would agree that not all the virtues in this passage are likely to be embodied in any one woman. Whew! That no doubt will bring you great relief. I would settle for one out of ten! But seriously, what are the standards by which we would be evaluated today? More importantly, what characteristics does God seek to instill in the lives of women in His family?

Demands placed on women have not remained static. Women served in diverse roles in every era, roles requiring a whole range of gifts and skills. Cultures, religions, and governments have determined customs and behavior of all members of a society. Today in many

Muslim countries, for example, women wear a veil and chador in compliance with the laws of Islam, while the free styles of American women vary wildly, depending upon the whim of the wearer. Downcast eyes of women of the lowest caste in India indicate their sense of self-worth. In earlier times women in Japan walked behind their husbands, symbolizing their subservience.

Suppose it were possible to call a women's summit in which women from Jesus' day met with us to compare our lives. We might be interested in how they got all their housekeeping chores done without a car, cell phone, or dishwasher. They probably would ask why we live such frantic lives, never stopping to enjoy our blessings and ruining our health in the meantime. Dorcas, however, might confess to coveting one invention of our day—the sewing machine. Faithful seamstress in her ministry to the poor of the first century, she would have reveled in an electric sewing machine with computer functions—and the electricity to power it. We, however, would express a longing for that era in Palestine. A simpler life, a quieter atmosphere, an escape from the chaos and complexity of our time.

Even within the last century American women have experienced enormous changes. And lest you believe that everything new has already been discovered and available at Wal-Mart, hold on to your hat. We've only just begun to experience the amazing speed of change—changes in technology, medicine, international configurations, and ethical and sociological factors—all of which will affect you.

In the context of certain change around us, we are aware that the role of women is also changing. More than half of the adult female population in our country is employed outside the home. The "glass ceiling" is slowly rising to make room for more women in management, and the salaries for women are inching toward equal pay. In most arenas we are seeing the positive difference when there is shared leadership and partnership between men and women. In these new opportunities we are increasingly aware of conflicts in time constraints, loyalties and responsibilities. New problems of domestic abuse, drug and alcohol addiction, AIDS, and violence swirl with the perennial problems of poverty and injustice to form new lethal potions bringing death to guilty and innocent alike. What will the future bring for women?

More important to us, how will Christian women respond to the challenges of the new century? God has placed inherent traits within women, timeless virtues, uniquely needed in these days. What does He require of women in His service? Do the courageous acts of women in the past give us instruction for today, or do we need a whole new set of responses?

God has always used hard times to perfect His people for great acts of obedience and courage. Challenges abound today and into the future, but God has invested special gifts in His daughters to be used at His pleasure. We are ready to step up to the plate and with intentionality—and the grace of God—claim the tasks for which we are uniquely gifted.

Where is that Proverbs superwoman when you need her? Honestly, though, I have a sneaky feeling that no one woman can do it all today any more than she could in Bible days. But with God's leadership and power, together we can meet this century's challenges and laugh with assurance at the time to come.

These Things
Never Happen to Men?

"I had done my homework," she said. "I thought I was prepared. But why did I dread it so much?"

I understood her discomfort. Talking about the "facts of life" had always been difficult for me, too. Born twenty years too soon, we lacked the advantage of a more open style in discussing sex. Teenagers hear so much now at school in sex education classes, but just as they did in my time, they probably still get most information from a less reliable source—each other.

"When I talked to my son," she said "I fast-forwarded to the actual delivery of a baby, armed with pictures and facts I had gotten from my doctor just for this purpose." When her son looked at the pictures of the birth, he winced. And then he asked, "Doesn't it hurt?"

"Well, yes, of course it hurts," she said, "but after it's all over, a mother forgets the pain in the joy of her baby."

Her son relaxed a bit, but then he straightened his shoulders and asked, "Are you sure it never happens to men?"

While modern medical miracles occur each year at an accelerating pace, no man has yet given birth to a child. Few men have chosen the role of woman in any case, and no wonder. In *Just Like a Woman*, Dianne Hales tells us that until the eighteenth century, "medical opinion saw the female body as a lesser variation on the male model, with analogous reproductive organs turned about and tucked inside."

Today the scientific revolution is replacing old stereotypes of women, and the differences between men and women are not seen as defects, damage, or disease. Hales writes, "We are gaining greater insight into womanly ways of creating and connecting, expressing emotion and finding spiritual . . . fulfillment."

Even as the birthing experience itself "never happens to men," other roles, challenges, and characteristics appear to fall largely into a woman's domain as well. Women generally assume the "nurturer" role, having the strong compulsion to fix things and to relieve ills. And today plenty of things need fixing. We need not worry about job security in the maternal role!

Days of Unparalleled Opportunity
Imagine life at the beginning of the twentieth century. In 1900:
• The United States had one-fourth of the people it has now, and none of them had ever flown.
• Highway accidents were rare (thirty-six in 1900).
• Some eight hundred thousand wives were in the work force; today approximately 34 million women juggle work and home responsibilities.
• Television and computers were the stuff of fiction.
• The average American family consisted of 4.8 people; in 1998 it had decreased in number to 2.6 people.

On December 7, 1941, life changed for all US citizens. My family had gone to the home of a family in our church for Sunday dinner. The children rushed through the meal to go outside to play. After sitting through Sunday School and church we needed to run off the accumulated energy. When we came back inside the house, the adults were still seated around the table, but their usual laughter and lively voices were missing. We soon knew the reason for their sober faces. Japan had bombed a military fleet resting in Pearl Harbor, Honolulu, Hawaii. Eighteen ships were destroyed and twenty-four hundred men were killed. The next morning President Franklin D. Roosevelt asked Congress to declare war on Japan. Germany and Italy honored their treaty with Japan by declaring war on the US, launching America into World War II.

As the men joined the armed forces, women at home took over their jobs in defense industries. Norman Rockwell pictured a young American woman in a factory on a magazine cover, and "Rosie the Riveter" became an image of national pride. Women working in different capacities—in defense plants and other jobs ordinarily held by men—kept things going at home. After the war ended and the men came home, some women continued working. Many more went home with their husbands and started a "baby boom," a generation which has since made its impact felt in every facet of life. Now that these "boomers" are approaching retirement age, they continue as a group to affect the economy, legislation, and certainly the future.

After 1945, Rosie the Riveter faded from memory, a historic anomaly. But in 1997, working women of World War II, including volunteers, received invitations to the Little White House in Warm Springs, Georgia, for special recognition. Out of that reunion the American Rosie the Riveter Association was reinstated, and on Pearl Harbor Day, 1998, the organization was incorporated.

By mid-twentieth century changes were accelerating. Television was not altogether common; in 1950 only nine percent of the households reported owning one. Today ninety-eight percent have one—or multiple—units. I remember well spending Christmas in the home of my "wealthy" aunt in 1952. I knew she was rich, because she owned a TV! The height of luxury was sitting for hours enthralled by the early programming. Later we bought a TV set for ourselves, and when reception was poor we, nevertheless, sat mesmerized by the "snow." Although technically better in production today, the programming of the Lawrence Welk Show, I Love Lucy, and the Ed Sullivan Show among others of those early days were hard to beat. Children could watch it all; nothing had to be rated for sexual or violent themes. My, how things have changed!

As with many of my age cohorts, I was the first in my family to be graduated from a university. The university catalog never carried a "For Men Only" designation, but most of the women self-selected out of a degree program leading toward any career other than secretary, teacher, or nurse. A few hardy souls defied custom and chose a different career goal, but most of us blithely took our path along the tried and true avenues.

Today college women choose study programs in every department and seldom have difficulty landing a job in any field because of their gender. Not only that, women can matriculate in any college or university, even a military institute. What once caused a stir with the news media—a woman in the military!—hardly raises an eyebrow. And women students can join freely in sports programs as well, including football, boxing and hockey. US News and World Report recently reported that ten years ago 132 high school girls participated in wrestling. In 2000 there were 2,474. It is possible that women will wrestle in the 2004 Olympics.

With the diversity in college offerings for girls, it

follows that new careers await the female graduate unlike any time before. Men train to fill teaching and nursing positions; women find fulfillment as construction workers and airplane pilots and doctors and lawyers and—anything they want. The choices are almost unlimited. The best-paying job for women today, according to the Bureau of Labor Statistics, is attorney, but the salary increase for nurses and teachers has done much to retain women who love those professions. According to David Bach's Smart Women Finish First, "working women currently earn more than $1 trillion a year and account for upwards of 52 percent of all earned household income in this country."

With the coming of women to leadership positions, new styles of management have developed. Women leaders prefer to listen and share ownership rather than to issue ultimatums and wield power from the top down. This style leads naturally to empowerment, openness, and motivation of employees. In Megatrends for Women, Naisbitt and Aburdene state, "Over time women have evolved a successful leadership style that rejects the military model in favor of supporting and empowering people. Male management guru Peter Drucker endorses it—because it works better than the old ways."

Voters in 2000 must have agreed, for they elected the largest number of women ever for Congress, thirteen in the Senate and sixty-seven in the House of Representatives. Politics is beginning to catch up with medicine, law, business, journalism, and other professions in the numbers of females in leadership.

Like men, women are reported to have improved health. Medical research, formerly focused exclusively on men, now includes women in research studies.

Results of the studies will enable physicians to prescribe more accurately for medication and treatment specifically for women. Life expectancy is now 79 years for women and 74 years for men, a dramatic increase since 1900 when the typical woman could expect to live until age 48.

Women hold greater wealth than ever before. According to the Internal Revenue Service, 35 percent of all estates valued at more than 5 million dollars are controlled by women. Approximately half of all small businesses in this country are female-owned.

To summarize, today women are better educated, employed more widely, live longer, and are healthier and wealthier to enjoy and make use of the last stage of life.

. . . And Days of Unprecedented Problems

Just at the time women are experiencing unparalleled opportunity in every way, we also face problems of unprecedented and consuming magnitude.

• **Addiction** both to alcohol and drugs remains a leading cause of concern to parents, schools, and society in general. It is a leading cause of crime. Babies born with fetal alcohol syndrome or addicted to drugs swell the infant death statistics. Many of the survivors present challenges to schools and society in general because of their severe and oppressive learning disabilities and emotional problems.

• **AIDS** has claimed 21.8 million lives worldwide since the epidemic began, including 9 million women and 4.3 million children under fifteen. While ninety-five percent of these statistics come from developing countries, the US is not problem-free. In January of 2001, AIDS was the leading cause of death for African Americans between the ages of twenty-five and forty-four, according to a report of the Centers for Disease Control.

• **Poverty**, although showing a decline in incidence in the 2000 census, still plagues too many people in our wealthy US. A large gap exists between median incomes among racial groups. Children under six continue to remain vulnerable. A study released February 2001 reported that one in five children (20.3 percent) lives in poverty. The 2000 census shows that those living with a mother but no father experience a poverty rate more than five times the rate for children in married-couple families.

• **Domestic violence** occurs more frequently than any other crime. Battering, the major cause of injury to women, results in more injuries to women than auto accidents, muggings, and rapes combined. The male batterer is much more likely to abuse his children as well.

• **Pornography** victimizes women and children. Its motive—the dollar. Its defense—constitutional freedom of the press. Invasion of the Internet is its latest tactic in getting into your home, and sexual content on television has risen sharply since 1997.

• **Teenage pregnancy** in the US exceeds that of all other developed countries. Of the approximate 1 million teenage pregnancies each year, ninety-five percent are unintended and almost one-third end in abortions, according to the National Center for Disease Prevention and Health Promotion.

• **Breakdown of the family** has resulted in a changing configuration of today's family unit. In a report issued by the US Census Bureau, one analyst writes, "High levels of divorce and postponement of first marriage are among the changes that have reshaped the living

arrangements of children and adults since the 1970s."
More unmarried and same-sex couples live together. As
a result, more than twice as many children are now living with one parent, eight times as many unmarried
couples are living together, and twice as many women
live alone.

• **International terrorism** has its grip on the world's
peoples. US citizens were still reeling from the
September 11 attack on the World Trade towers and
the Pentagon when the fear of anthrax and biochemi-
cal warfare escalated our terror and rage. Though ini-
tially staged in this country, it is a threat to every
country—a war unlike any fought before. Faceless
adversaries in borderless regions defy the proven strate-
gies of warfare. Once again, women gear up for new
roles and responsibilities.

As long as this laundry list of problems is, we could
add others: care of the elderly, prison overcrowding,
personal and corporate bankruptcy, public education
quality, bio-engineering, health care cost control, and
more.

How can we possibly take all this in? Must we be
burdened by the mountain of information? No, but we
must live in recognition of it. God has uniquely prepared women to be yoked along with men to be His
emissaries in a very needy world.

Next Level—Equal Partnership
The game is heating up. The players in the game are
courageously struggling against formidable odds. It
seems strange, but a large part of the team is still in the
dugout—more than half the team, as a matter of fact.
They cheer and keep the crowd apprised of the game
statistics, and seem to be passionately interested in the

game. But why doesn't the coach get them in the game? Are they on the team or not?

We women wear the uniform and attend the workouts, but few of us play in the game. Not because we are not capable, not dedicated, not eager to play, but because. . . . Men in the past have thought women to be incompetent, condemned to be under the domination of men, paying the debt for Eve's sin. Others have seen us as a treasure to be preserved, a fragile thing to be protected. As women we have been timid to step up to the plate, unwilling to be considered contentious or to break out of our subservient role.

Today, however, the need for a united effort of men and women is urgent. We know ourselves to be ready for service, neither fragile nor inept, but committed to the task given to the church—a task challenging enough for a whole team effort. Women alone are not able, any more than men alone, to shoulder the problems of our day. Some men speak of the danger of a "takeover" by women. They worry about the competition women will bring. A man friend teasingly once told me, "Women don't play fair. They always get to the meeting on time, have all their materials ready at hand, and make well thought out contributions." A pastor at another time said, "I like women. Why, some of my best men are women." Certainly, history has brought massive change in our relationships with men. I tend to agree with Dianne Hales' conclusion:

> Some call the silent revolution that has structured modern culture "feminization;" others see it as long-overdue normalization. I think of it as humanization, the stretching of a man-sized world into a universe large and deep enough to accommodate

the perspectives and potential of two similar but distinct sexes. Whatever the name, it's taking some getting used to.

In this book we face the challenge of becoming an equal partner in dealing with the issues of the day. We will be confronted with tasks we must accept and things we need to lay aside. Being affirmed for what we have done well, we will take a look at opportunities we have and the spiritual resources that are ours.

Timeless Virtues for Twenty-first Century Women

Many women struggle today with past failures that hinder their moving on into a happy and fulfilled present and future. Having been forgiven by God, they regularly open the wounds again and again and wallow in the mire of guilt. But God wants more for His daughters than despair. Forgetting what lies behind, Christian women can move forward in joy and peace.

Two people—a married couple perhaps?—trudged the road to Emmaus, as we are told in Luke 24:13. They spoke softly, as though they lacked the energy for more. Occasionally they wiped tears from their saddened eyes. The grieving pair mirrored the emotions of many that day, and for good reason. Jesus was crucified and their hopes had died with Him. The past, a waste: their future—who could say what torments it held? One quietly joined them in their own via dolorosa and His words breathed new life into their being. Later, in the breaking of the word and the bread, the resurrected Jesus transformed sadness into rejoicing, despair into confidence, defeat into victory.

For the women among Jesus' followers, relief came

much earlier that day. They were last at the Cross, first at the tomb, and first to encounter the living Christ. Throughout Christ's ministry they worked behind the scenes to advance His work. Never seeking recognition, they also never shirked the task. Even at the Cross they agonized with Christ's mother. And when they appeared at the burial site to prepare His body, a woman's job, He honored their faithfulness by His appearance.

Two thousand years later, we modern women, facing completely different circumstances, commit our loyalty to the risen Christ. He has gifted us with all necessary virtues for the task. Strange, we see that they are not new, though the day is. They are instead the enduring qualities that fit the women to walk with him those centuries ago.

We remind ourselves that the gift comes from the Father and is not of our own making: "Not that we are competent of ourselves to claim anything as coming from us; our competence is from God, who has made us competent to be ministers of a new covenant, not in a written code but in the Spirit; for the written code kills, but the Spirit gives life" (2 Corinthians 3:5–6).

We thank God, therefore, for the competencies He places within us, and submit them to His use. May we find new strength for these new days in Him.

CHAPTER 1

Overcoming Obstacles

> *Oh, what a happy child I am*
> *Though I cannot see!*
> *I am resolved that in this world*
> *Contented I will be.*
> *How many blessings I enjoy*
> *That other people don't!*
> *So don't weep or sigh, because I'm blind,*
> *I cannot, nor I won't.*

Fannie Crosby was just eight years old when she wrote this, her first poem. A doctor's tragic mistake had claimed her sight when she was only six weeks old, yet during her lifetime she wrote 2000 hymns sharing her faith and commitment to her Lord. We, too, glimpse the Almighty God when we sing, "To God Be the Glory," "Blessed Assurance," "Redeemed," "All the Way My Savior Leads Me," and many of her other hymns. Miss Crosby has been the subject of countless sermons and devotionals, and rightly so. Today we stand in awe of her grace in difficult circumstances.

Fannie Crosby is one in a constant flow of women who have exemplified such courage. In fact, women's ability to overcome barriers is one thing that makes us special. Living the abundant life in Christ entails risk, and encountering obstructions along the way is inevitable. While we have only limited choice in the challenges of life, we determine for ourselves how we will meet them.

Obstacles Along the Way

In early 1963, my husband Bill and I were appointed as music missionaries in Indonesia. We were to live on the beautiful island of Java. (Yes, they do grow coffee there.) Our two little daughters, aged eight and three, and soon-to-be-born baby son were going with us to this faraway land. We were thrilled to be going to serve the Lord in this way!

When we received instructions for the preparations we needed to make, we thought it could not possibly be done. The official paperwork seemed endless and complicated. We bought the suggested items for life in Indonesia, including a kerosene cooking stove and a four-year supply of toilet tissue. Do you have *any* idea how much toilet tissue you use in four years? After acquiring the things we might need, we then struggled to get it all in a regulation-size crate—something like mashing a pillow into a shoebox. Getting immunizations, ordering schoolbooks, storing unneeded belongings—it seemed impossible.

Then suddenly one day it was done. After telling our family goodbye—the most difficult task of all—we flew out of Love Field in Dallas, Texas, headed for Hawaii and the Philippines where we would await our visas to Indonesia.

In June 1963, we arrived in Bandung, Indonesia, the city where we would study the language. A few months later, our little family made a trip to visit our assigned station in the city of Semarang, in Central Java. We still were not totally acclimated to our new home.

We knew that although the distance was only 250 miles, it would take us about 12 hours. The traffic was congested—not with cars and trucks, but ox carts, pedicabs, and pedestrians. We drove a Chevrolet station wagon, provided by the mission. The drive was hot and long. Our two little daughters tired of the books and toys they had brought along and began to whine the complaint of all little travelers through time, "How much longer 'til we get there?" Even their baby brother was weary of being held (no car seats for babies either).

Somewhere along the way, we came to a bridge with a huge sign at its entrance. In large block letters it read: *Jembatan ini sangat dikuatirkan.* Although we weren't skilled with the Indonesian language, we understood enough to know that safe passage over this bridge was seriously doubted.

We looked around for someone to tell us how dangerous it would be, but we saw no one. What should we do? Stay true to the course and risk the journey or seek a safer detour? Finally, urgency trumped caution and we inched slowly and safely across the bridge.

All of us have encountered obstacles in our Christian pilgrimage that make the journey difficult and challenging. We may be surprised by failure in marriage or disappointments in the lives of our children. When illness or tragedy enters our lives, we struggle to find meaning. In entering the job market, we may meet discrimination up close, both in hiring and salaries. We are more often victims of abuse than men, and we are most vulnerable when tragedy strikes.

Some hindrances simply delay our journey or cause inconvenience. Other more serious obstacles, however, stop us in our tracks. The devastating impact may last throughout the rest of our lives.

The Hemorrhaging Woman

"If a woman has a discharge of blood for many days, not at the time of her impurity, or if she has a discharge beyond the time of her impurity, all the days of the discharge she shall continue in uncleanness; as in the days of her impurity, she shall be unclean." (Leviticus 15:25) These words from the Torah had plagued her almost all her life. At first, in her earlier years, she had been merely inconvenienced five days each month when her menstrual cycle forced her into the "unclean" designation. She chafed at the indignities this physiological reality heaped upon her; she hadn't chosen to be a girl! But at least she was in the company of other women and it was only temporary—until the next month.

The last decade, however, had brought her to the brink of disaster—physically, financially, emotionally, and spiritually. Physically, the twelve years had taken its toll. Anemia, brought on by the constant loss of life-giving blood, left her weak and almost helpless. She had sought help from doctors near and far, but the only visible result was depletion of financial resources. No one had diagnosed the illness correctly, but many had recommended costly cures and treatments to no avail.

Her greatest loss, however, was her place in the community. Close friends now passed her on the street and turned their heads without a hint of recognition. On good days she understood and forgave them. After all, the penalty for touching an unclean person, or even sitting on her chair, was great for Israelites (Leviticus 15).

She had no comfort from the covenant people. She was barred from attending any gathering for fear of contaminating others. Her own husband was forbidden to express his love for her—if any still existed. It had been *twelve years*, after all. Perhaps he had already taken another woman. How could a God who cared about her let such an injustice escape His notice? (Find this story in Luke 8:43–48.)

Susan Ray's Story

Cecil and Charlene Ray were the picture of a dedicated, successful pastor and wife in West Texas in the early 1950s. Everything about their family fit the ideal of the day: father and mother, two children, boy and girl. The church was growing, and all seemed well until February 27, 1952. Frances Riley tells their story in *The King's Daughter Dances*. On that morning Charlene awakened to the cry of their four-year-old daughter, Susan. She rushed to her room and found her kicking her legs violently. "My back hurts!" When they were able to get Susan to the doctor, he advised immediate hospitalization.

The spinal tap confirmed the doctor's worst fears: polio. Not yet knowing the diagnosis, the Rays watched in terror as a medical team gave frantic attention to Susan's breathing. With the sudden appearance of Lubbock firemen, iron lung in tow, the Rays reeled with the realization that their little daughter's condition was indeed critical. Susan had respiratory polio. In the early years of the polio epidemic in America, firemen were the primary group trained to use and maintain iron lungs.

In 1950, polio had exploded into the worst epidemic in American history. In 1953, some 35,000 people were stricken. Parents worked feverishly to protect their children, the favored prey of this illness. They sterilized objects at home, avoided contacts outside the home, especially swimming pools, parks, and theaters. They postponed surgeries during June through September, months when the incidence of polio was greatest. Nothing seemed to stem the tide of this ruthless enemy.

When the disease had run its course in little Susan's body, she had escaped death's clutches but her life would never be the same, nor would her family's. The iron lung, like a knight's armor, offered safe haven but restricted mobility. Cecil and his partners, the firemen, later created new and more effective iron lungs that enabled Susan and many others to survive polio and live for many years.

But what kind of life would Susan experience? This beautiful child would never again romp and play with her friends. She could never know freedom from the respirator that kept her alive. Going to school was out of the question. If she lived to be an adult, what could she possibly do day after day? If she should outlive her mother and father, who would take care of her? Surely such outstanding Christian parents deserved a special act of God. Couldn't He have intervened in Susan's case?

My Story
Just as Susan's life-changing misfortune began suddenly, so did mine. Early on a Saturday morning in September of 1998, I awakened with the strange feeling all was not well. If pressed to be more specific with my complaint, it seemed to be a weakness in my right leg. "Just need a cup of coffee," I thought. My right foot caught on the edge of every stair on my way to the kitchen.

It was to have been a joyful day, a time of reunion with my husband Bill, who had been in Indonesia for two weeks. He had gone there to co-lead a workshop on conflict transformation. The workshop included Christian, Muslim, Hindu, and Buddhist leaders who sought training in this very relevant issue, not knowing that tragic "holy wars" between Muslims and Christians would erupt only months later.

Bill was on his way home. He had telephoned the

day before when he arrived in Los Angeles. I had written down the expected time of his arrival, underscored it, and put an exclamation mark after it. After forty-five years of marriage, neither of us relished the times apart. But we would be together again soon. I couldn't wait!

The nagging feeling that something was wrong refused to go away even after a cup of coffee. Finally, though it was still early, I called our son Ross who lived only five minutes away.

"Ross, I don't feel well."

"I'm coming," he responded.

In the emergency room, medical personnel began their usual diagnostic routine. When Bill arrived later in the day, he was met with the news that I had had a light stroke, a brain attack. By Sunday the paralysis had left my right side totally useless. The following days were filled with physical, occupational, speech, and recreational therapy and continued tests. After two and a half weeks in the hospital, I went home in a wheel-chair with braces on my ankle and knee.

Further therapy in the next months was designed to increase mobility on my right side. I supplemented my speech therapy by reading out loud. Psalms would be a good choice, I thought. My articulation did improve, but I had not planned for the spiritual exercise it became. Frankly, in the past I read some Psalms and thought the Israelites must have been chronic complainers. Now I joined voice and heart with them:

"I cry to you, O Lord;
I say, 'You are my refuge,
my portion in the land of the living'
Give heed to my cry, for I am brought very low."
(Psalm 142:5–6)

Day after day the Psalms gave me voice to ask God's blessing and to be assured that He loved me.

From the time of hospitalization news spread quickly to friends everywhere, and they prayed for my recovery. Would I ever walk again? Use my right hand to write and play the piano? Speak and teach before groups? Even with therapy, no one would predict. "We don't know. We'll just have to wait to see," was my doctor's prognosis. Bill and so many others prayed for total recovery, that I would return to my normal life. I would gladly have received such an answer.

God has such a wonderful sense of humor! One day a cartoon fell out of my Bible. It pictured a bearded man dressed in a robe of Bible times. The placard he carried proclaimed, "The end is *not* near. You must learn to cope!" I could not remember when or why I had clipped it and put it in my Bible, but there it was. It seemed to say, "You're going to be all right. Now get up and work!" It's still in my Bible, bearing the same message.

Meeting Obstacles

These three women, each in a different way, are representative of countless others who have met situations that have threatened their lives and redefined their future. None of us chose our mishap. Some might say we just had bad luck. Others might look for more profound reasons that bad things happen to good people. Car accidents, serious illnesses, and intentional attacks by others leave victims in the wake, women as well as men.

Both to the woman "with an issue of blood" and to Susan Ray the future looked bleak, years filled with unknown horrors and fears. I felt that life-changing calamities happened to other people, not me. Funny how one never considers herself a likely character in a tragedy.

Do you have acquaintances or close friends who are presently experiencing traumas that rob them of normal activity or threaten their lives? Perhaps you have a condition that limits your mobility, or are dealing with a situation so difficult that it has crowded out every other concern. You know the pain and heartache of a wounded sojourner.

While physical handicaps are obvious, other disabilities lie deeply and silently within the hearts and minds of their victims. Victims of child or spousal abuse and rape are often unable to move beyond the pain of their past to find a happy and productive life. Illiteracy or discrimination cripples others. Many face a future without hope or promise of release. If life were a merry-go-round, they would definitely want to get off. How does a Christian woman overcome the obstacles that seem to stand in her way?

Perhaps we can learn from each other. By considering how other Christian women have dealt with obstacles, perhaps we can find help in dealing with our own.

She Touched Him

The story of the hemorrhaging woman is found in Luke 8:43-50. She had all but lost heart when she heard of a man called Jesus who was said to perform miracles. Not only had He healed many who were ill, He had even raised the dead. Her heart must have beat faster each time she thought, "If it's true, He can certainly do something for me! It's surely worth a try." She had heard that Jesus had returned to her city and determined to seek Him out. When she found Him, He was in the middle of a huge crowd. She edged her way in, unconcerned that she was ceremonially contaminating everyone she touched.

As she got nearer to Jesus, she could hear His conversation with Jairus, the synagogue leader and neighborhood's high official. Apparently, he was leading Jesus to his dying daughter. She could sense the urgency in Jairus' voice as he fell at Jesus' feet and begged for Him to please come quickly. When they hurried off, she saw her opportunity slipping away. "No, no, don't leave!" her silent scream seemed to tear her apart, but the unaware men continued on their way.

And then she did a shameful thing. Against all teachings of the day, she touched Jesus. It was just the fringe of His garment, but it was enough. In that exact instant she felt the flow of blood cease. She was healed!

"Who touched me?"

His disciples went into a frenzy. "Who touched you, Master?" How could they know in such a crowd? Those standing by quickly denied any guilt.

"Not I!" "I didn't do it." "It sure wasn't me."

Jesus knew that power had gone out from Him, and He knew why. When the woman realized she was found out, she fearfully confessed that she had touched Jesus. Jesus' words brought added relief, "Daughter, your faith has made you well; go in peace." No longer was she an outcast. Jesus had called her daughter! She was clean!

She Served God

For months after Susan Ray's diagnosis of polio, her life hung in the balance. Each crisis seemed to challenge her parents' belief that she would not only survive but would serve God with her life. Cecil's expertise with machinery enabled him to adjust the iron lung so that Susan would receive the proper amount of oxygen.

Gradually Susan's condition improved, and when she was six she attended public school as a homebound student in her own home. While she could never be free for active play with children, many friends came to her house to play, and her brother, Lanny, was her closest playmate.

When they moved to San Antonio for Cecil's new work, no homebound teacher was available, so Charlene became Susan's instructor. She continued to teach her until Susan reached junior high, when others offered their teaching services.

Susan attended church services regularly and especially enjoyed learning about missionaries. No one, however, could have predicted her response at a Christian conference in New Mexico when Susan was eleven years old. The speaker concluded his message with an appeal to those who felt God was calling them to missionary service. Susan asked a friend to push her chair to the front of the auditorium. She was responding to a call for missionaries.

Some in attendance that night must have questioned the wisdom of God's call to little Susan. But others who knew her well were profoundly touched by this brave girl's decision. In *The King's Daughter Dances*, Frances Riley writes, "For each of those making decisions that day, life held many roadblocks and challenges, but not as many as would face Susan as she worked out her calling. Here was a missionary volunteer who could not sit erect, walk, or even breathe on her own; Susan was a respiratory quadriplegic, almost totally paralyzed by polio!"

When Susan died of pneumonia on February 27, 1995, she had lived for forty-three years, tied with a fragile tether to her respirators. And what of her call to missions? Susan made full use of her abilities by writing books and numerous articles that required study and research. She wrote three books in collaboration with her father. She taught children in her church and in the Spanish mission. Her many interests in politics, social issues, current events, and archaeology committed her to social action. In spite of limited mobility in her hands, she cross-stitched samplers and made Christmas cards with contrivances engineered by her father.

Most important of all, Susan lived her life in Christ to the extreme limits of her capability. At one time Susan, reflecting on the life of President Franklin Roosevelt, said, "I think first of a great president of the United States and only second as a person with handicaps. I would far rather be remembered for what I can contribute than for having handicaps." Susan certainly achieved her desire.

I Sought God
Three years after the stroke my rehab is still continuing, but with less-than-hoped-for results. I have chosen to be positive, but some days discouragement comes unbidden. "Hurry, honey, we're going to be late to church. Grab your Bible,"—and my cane. Never leave home without it. Lack of strength and dexterity on my right side prohibits my doing simple tasks, like opening a package of crackers or fastening clothing or jewelry. "Would you please cut my meat?" The question is hard for a grown woman to ask.

But wait; lest you think this is a huge obstacle, let me tell you this is the greatest adventure of my life. While others prayed for my total recovery, I was led to pray that God would give me the ability to do all He wanted me to do.

After four months I returned to work part-time. My ten years as executive director of Woman's Missionary Union, the largest Protestant women's organization in the world, had taken me throughout the US and even around the world. Travel would be limited at first, but after a few months I picked up an almost normal schedule. God be praised!

In September 1999, at the age of sixty-six, I retired. My busy life would be over; my days of meaningful service were behind me—I thought. Instead I finished writing one book and began another. My church remembered my words, "When I retire, there will be more time," and gave me plenty to do. Invitations to speak continued, even from far-off places. So much for retirement! We never outlive our usefulness to God. The sphere of activity and mode of service may change, but God always graciously allows His children a part in His Kingdom's work.

The greatest blessing of all undoubtedly has been the devoted care of my husband, Bill. Our love was sure and strong, but a heavy burden can test the mettle of any relationship. Each of us, though bonded together in marriage for forty-five years, was very independent and pulled his or her own weight. In the middle of the night, while I was still in the hospital, I began to list in my mind the things I could no longer do. I would put such a heavy burden on Bill! I neglected to factor in his servant heart. His commitment years ago "to love and honor through sickness and health" was not just a vocal exercise, it was a commitment meant to last a lifetime. Again, I was blessed.

Bill was a strength for me even in the hospital. After my condition was stabilized I was moved to the rehab floor dubbed "Easy Street." (My doctor said it would be anything but easy!) Days were filled with taxing therapy, but evenings brought time with Bill. Occasionally he brought dinner, a welcome change from hospital food. If the weather was nice, he wheeled me outside for fresh air. Each night he would go to sleep in his chair, holding my hand, a visible sign that visiting hours were over for me. Then he would kiss me goodnight and leave my hospital room. On the TV set in my room was a closed-circuit channel from the lobby. As Bill approached the doors leading outside, he would turn to the camera and throw me a kiss. I always wondered if other patients tuned into the lobby channel thought that kiss was for them.

No longer will I be able to accompany Bill at the piano. Since college days, we have enjoyed making music together, he with his beautiful Irish tenor voice and I on the piano. But I'm so grateful for the years I could! When the first sense of self-pity comes, it is quickly followed by a wave of determination. So many people with less mobility than I have are busy in God's work, cheerfully serving Him. I have the best life partner in the world and children and grandchildren who bring us both great joy. What more could I want? God is so good!

How Do We Overcome Obstacles?
Christian women meet adversity in different ways. The woman with the issue of blood in Luke's Gospel had known what it meant to be ostracized by friends and an outcast in the religious community. She was relieved of her burden by Jesus Himself. As she reached out to Jesus, He gave her the healing she sought. The Great Physician once again brought new life.

No doubt Susan Ray's parents prayed for complete

recovery for their daughter as well. In spite of the fervency of their plea, Susan remained a respiratory quadriplegic for the rest of her life. Miracle healing was not the way God chose to answer their prayers. God apparently had another plan for Susan's life. He would equip her and her parents with incredible wisdom, courage and faith.

Others might have refused to accept the challenge. Sometimes it seems easier to give up and just blame God for an impossible situation. When obstacles enter our lives, they come accompanied by a choice: we can overcome the obstacles or let them overcome us.

The Lincoln Center in New York City was the scene of a moving event on November 18, 1995, where the great violinist Itzhak Perlman performed. Perlman gives a brilliant display of courage before he even begins a performance. Stricken with polio as a child, he wears braces on his feet and legs. He walks with crutches across the stage, sits down in his chair, slowly puts his crutches on the floor, and unclasps the braces on his legs. Then he takes his violin, puts it under his chin, and nods his readiness to the conductor. The audience sits quietly, almost reverently, during this ritual.

This evening, just as Perlman finished the first few bars, a string on his violin broke. Expecting a delay in the performance, the audience was surprised when he closed his eyes, then signaled to the conductor to begin again. He played the remainder of the selection with passion, power, and purity. He performed the entire symphony on just three strings, modulating and recomposing the piece in his mind. When he finished, the audience sat in awed silence. Then they rose and cheered in profound appreciation for what they had seen and heard.

Perlman smiled, wiped his brow, and raised his bow to quiet the crowd. "You know," he said in a quiet, pensive tone, "sometimes it is the artist's task to find out how much music you can still make with what you have left."

You know others who continue to live effective, productive lives in spite of difficult circumstances. Paul says in his letter to the Corinthian Christians: "Therefore I am content with weaknesses, insults, hardships, persecutions, and calamities for the sake of Christ; for whenever I am weak, then I am strong" (2 Corinthians 12:10).

Susan used her weakness and exchanged it for God's perfecting power. We marvel at her accomplishments. Writing books, relating to people individually and in groups, assuming a leadership role in a Spanish mission, taking the initiative in matters of social justice—who would have imagined that Susan could achieve so much in spite of her limitations! Again, God provided His strength as she worked through her weaknesses.

It is possible also to work *with our weaknesses*. Bill prayed that I would have recover from my stroke, but I was led to pray differently. While I worked hard to regain the full use of my right hand and leg, I wanted to be sensitive to what God was doing. My prayer, therefore, has been, "Lord, give me whatever skills I need to accomplish what You still want me to do for You."

The tag on my car and the cane both identify my condition: handicapped. A child pulls on his mother's skirttail as he mouths the words, "What's wrong with that lady?" Some move back to give me more room, while others rush to get out of the way. Many people offer help, but more often they do not know how. It's a new experience for me to receive help, being more comfortable as the helper. I think, however, a passage in Romans gives helpful instruction to all who suffer: "We also boast in our sufferings, knowing that suffering produces endurance, and endurance produces character, and character produces hope, and hope does not disappoint us, because God's love has been poured into our hearts through the Holy Spirit that has been given to us" (Rom. 5:3–5).

The first gift of suffering is *endurance*. Another translation is *fortitude*. One list of fortitude's synonyms includes *grit* and *guts*. Fortitude allows us not only to passively endure but also to actively overcome the attacks we experience. It puts starch in our backbone.

Next, "endurance produces *character*," Paul tells us. The Greek word translated "character" refers to metal that has been refined to make it pure and sterling. When suffering does its appointed work, a person becomes purer and more Christlike. Paul wrote to his beloved church at Philippi, "I want to know Christ and the power of his resurrection and the sharing of his sufferings by becoming like him in his death" (Philippians 3:10). Christ stands ready to make us like Him through suffering if we allow Him to do so.

Next, "character produces *hope*," the kind of hope that never disappoints. It is the hope that the ancient prophet, Isaiah, knew:
"Those who hope in the Lord will renew their strength.
They will soar on wings like eagles;
They will run and not grow weary,
They will walk and not be faint." (Isaiah 40:31 NIV)

Life's journey is sometimes interrupted by bridges marked, "Safe passage is seriously doubted." Trust God to provide safety in the crossing and to equip you with fortitude, character, and hope.

CHAPTER 2

Forgiving Others

Forgive and ask to be forgiven;
excuse rather than accuse.
Reconciliation begins first,
not with others but ourselves.
It starts with having a clean heart within.
A clean heart is able to see God in others.
We must radiate God's love.
—Mother Teresa, from her book
The Joy in Living

A little nine-year-old girl wept hot tears. Her father had left her! In the years following the divorce she learned of the many times her mother had shielded her and her older sister from the ugly truth, the sordid affairs of their father. Then the new wife issued an ultimatum—her or the girls. She never saw him after that, but she thinks about him often. As an adult, she has forgiven him and prays for him.

•••••

On a Saturday morning, a father and his daughter were driving to work out at the gym. With a green light they moved out into a major intersection. An eighteen-wheeler charged through the red light, broadsiding the helpless father and child. On impact, the car burst into flames. The man and his daughter perished at the scene, leaving wife and mother with grief untold. "The truck driver was just a young man," the widow recalls.

"Now for the remainder of his life he will bear this terrible memory." She forgave him early on. "His act was not malicious. It was just poor judgment and inexperience. I don't know where he is. I only pray that he has found some way to deal with it."

• • • • •

The parents had experienced their share of disappointment and anxiety with their teenage son in. From drugs to petty theft, he tried all manner of illegal activity.

When he suddenly showed up with a wife, they thought perhaps now he would settle down. He tried, but his addiction to drugs was more than he could handle. Now, he is in hiding, running from multiple charges, including writing checks on his parents' account. Have they been able to forgive him?

"Forgiveness is an advance payment. We have long since settled that. But we are still prayerful and concerned over continuing problems."

• • • • •

The young woman had been married five years when the relationship turned sour. She tried harder to please him, even quitting her job to have more time for him. Only later did she discover the cause of his alienation. He had found someone else he thought could supply all his needs, and he wanted to be free. Fortunately, she had marketable skills and could support herself after the divorce. She forgave him, but she never again entrusted her heart to a man.

• • • • •

It may be that one of these is your story. For years you have continued to feel the pain. Just when it seems to lie dormant for a season, old memories flood in and you remember what it was like before and how much you have lost. Much of what you have become today you blame on the hurt you endured then. Support groups designed to help adult children of alcoholics, victims of sexual abuse, and divorcees demonstrate the lingering effects of disappointment and abandonment. The best present you ever gave yourself is to let go of it—*forgive*!

Lewis Smedes says in his book, *Forgive and Forget: Healing the Hurts We Don't Deserve*: "Forgiving is love's toughest work, and love's biggest risk. If you twist it into something it was never meant to be, it can make you a doormat or an insufferable manipulator.... Forgiveness seems almost unnatural. Our sense of fairness tells us people should pay for the wrong they do. But forgiving is love's power to break natural rule."

First, we have to know what forgiveness is *not*. Forgiving someone is not denying the fact that he or she has hurt you or that what was done is all right. To the contrary, the Christian acknowledges the wrongdoing for what it is.

Secondly, forgiveness is not forgetting. We cannot carry deep hurts and suddenly blow them away like ripe dandelion plumes. We still bear the loss but not the hate. The very act of forgiveness transforms our hearts.

Thirdly, forgiveness does not depend on reconciliation. It is saying you forgive them and want to make things right between you. If the statement of forgiveness issues out of an honest and humble heart, you have faithfully fulfilled the command to forgive. Suppose the offender ignores your outstretched hand. She refuses to assume her part of the guilt and will not accept your offer of pardon. You are free. Forgiving others for their trespasses, you now receive God's forgiveness for your sins. Reconciliation between the two of you may or may not take place.

A few years ago, millions of viewers were transfixed by the brilliant portrayal of a hardened criminal. *Dead Man Walking* told the true story of Robert Lee Willie, who received a death sentence for kidnapping, raping, and murdering an 18-year-old girl. The movie mentions that he had kidnapped and raped others—one of them was Debbie Morris, who later authored the book *Forgiving the Dead Man Walking*.

Debbie's anguish did not end even after her kidnapper was caught and sentenced to death. Despite those who urged her to "get on with her life," her emotional ordeal continued. When Debbie found the grace to forgive Robert Willie on the day he was to be executed, she finally knew release from suffering. In prayer—for herself and for Willie—she discovered that only God's grace is sufficient.

As difficult as forgiveness is in such cases, its freeing power brings peace to the victim. People in treatment centers and support groups for victims of rape and sexual abuse are encouraged to work toward forgiveness. Counselors provide them with the necessary tools. Dr. Anne Davis, former Dean of the Carver School of Church and Social Work, now serves in a counseling agency in Waco, Texas that deals primarily with victims of crime, especially crimes of sexual abuse and rape. "The youngest victim of child sexual abuse we have seen was two months old. The oldest victim of rape was ninety-six." What part does forgiveness play in their counseling? "If the victim is able to forgive the perpetrator," reports Dr. Davis, "healing comes much faster."

Forgiveness in a Nation

Enmity within the population of the US is mirrored throughout the entire globe. Most wars being fought today are not between countries. They are instead waged within nations, between opposing ethnic or religious groups. Arab and Jew in the Middle East. Protestant and Catholic in the Emerald Isle. Christian and Muslim in Indonesia. Differences between such factions result in destruction of homes, disruption of lives, injuries, and deaths. Peacekeeping efforts, peace summits, and weapons agreements have limited success. One experiment offers a potential model for reconciliation.

South Africa has had a long history of racial divisiveness and human rights violations under apartheid. *Apartheid* means "separateness" in the Afrikaans language. It describes the rigid racial division between the governing white minority population and the nonwhite majority population. Opposition to the gross inequities and oppression of the nonwhite people finally forced them to fight for reforms. Urban revolts erupted, and as external pressure on South Africa intensified, the apartheid policies began to unravel. In 1990, a new president, F. W. de Klerk, proclaimed a formal end to apartheid.

The country then faced its greatest challenge: confronting the past to bring justice without creating a bloodbath of retaliation. Gratefully, the historic election of President Nelson Mandela and other leaders passed without the feared violence. Mandela, leader of the black opposition to the oppressive rule of the white minority, spent eighteen years in prison. During his time of captivity, Mandela became a worldwide symbol of resistance to white domination.

As a means of dealing with its past, South African leaders formed a Truth and Reconciliation Commission, chaired by Archbishop Desmond Tutu. The commission's purpose was twofold: to bring out the truth of the past and to foster reconciliation between members of its divided population.

The first objective required a complete investigation and clarification of human rights violations between 1960 and 1993, including the perspectives of the victims. Second, persons who made full disclosure of their involvement were granted amnesty. Third, victims personally testified of the human rights violations directed toward them and gave recommendations for reparation. Fourth, all records were compiled, and a comprehensive account recommended measures to prevent future violations of human rights.

The meeting of victim and perpetrator often resulted in emotional outbursts. The direct confrontation, however, allowed personal participation in the legal process by both. Much was learned in the process that can be applied in another setting.

Jubilee

Another international attempt to move toward reconciliation has to do with forgiveness, not of a person or a nation, but of debt. Many impoverished nations carry high levels of debt, usually due to shortsighted or profiteering leaders. Recognizing that many of these debts are unpayable and place an unreasonable toll on the country, the Jubilee 2000 Campaign called for a return to the biblical principle of Jubilee.

The Old Testament tells how God instructed Israel to establish a Jubilee year every fifty years, when slaves were freed and property returned to its original owner or his family (see Leviticus 25). In the year 2000 A.D., the spirit of Jubilee was reinstated in order to bring debt relief. Sixteen of the twenty-two countries included in the proposed program spent more on debt service payments than on health care. Canceling the debts of the world's most impoverished countries "will remove a major impediment to poverty reduction and economic growth and give these countries a fresh start in the new millennium."

As nations seek peaceful ways to resolve conflict and work together to solve mutual problems, we will enjoy a safer world. We women must pray that it will happen. Pray, too, for more women to enter the governmental and diplomatic posts.

On a visit to Russia in 1984 as the guests of the Russian Protestant Church, we were taken among other places to a new department store. After we had walked through the aisles and paid proper compliments to our hosts for the fine store, our small group waited at the car for the rest of the group. When an old woman, a street worker, approached us, our translator told her we were guests visiting from America. With that she dropped her broom and threw her arms around me.

"Please, miss, we do not want war with America. Please tell your president we don't want to fight." I quickly returned the embrace and assured her we did not want war either. Somehow I think that if women such as this were in the high political places, they would look to find creative approaches to settle international disputes.

Boys and Girls

As an elementary school teacher, one of my clear roles was as judge over the students' disputes. I was always interested in the different ways boys and girls behaved in their conflicts.

Generally, girls preferred to resolve their differences themselves. Quietly, but with great intensity, they confronted one another out of my earshot. I usually discovered an argument was brewing when another girl reported it. Arguments between boys were a different matter. They shouted at each other and were often in a full physical fight before I could arrive on the scene. In most cases girls resorted to tears, the boys to fists. For both boys and girls, the teacher's job was to facilitate an agreement, or at least a truce.

Unfortunately, we never totally master the art of living together amicably. Differences of opinion arise in the closest relationships. Harsh words or icy silence bruise a friendship. We feign indifference, but our hearts hurt with the loss of something special. We yearn for reconciliation, but we are often unwilling to let go of our pride and willfulness enough to seek it.

Women and Conflict

Do women handle conflict better than men? Are Christian women better able to forgive than non-Christian women?

The latter part of my professional life was spent not with children but with adult women. My daughter Erin, unaware that I was considering a big career leap, threw light on this matter as I decided about this new position. She was an administrative assistant in a large law firm, assigned to a female attorney.

"Mom, it's just been awful this week. Nothing I did was right. She's just been impossible. Wouldn't you hate to have to work altogether with women?"

Bingo! The search committee of Woman's

Missionary Union, the largest Protestant organization for women in the world, had just contacted me. The WMU staff consisted primarily of women, with something over a "tithe" of men. Its work was directed mainly toward girls and women, and its board was made up exclusively of women. I had worked largely with women as teacher and administrator of elementary schools for years, but this new position would place me in an almost exclusively woman's world. Would I hate working altogether in that milieu as my daughter had suggested? Would the fact that these women were committed Christians make a difference, or did they suffer from PMS like others of our gender?

After a decade of serving this outstanding organization, I have found answers to these questions, but they tend to be "yes, but—," "no, except when—," and "sometimes, but not always—." Just as the little girls in my first-grade classroom handled conflict differently from the boys, women and men vary in their reactions to disagreements. Women still resort to tears (worse in the PMS days) and men are more overt in their conflict. But those of us who have chosen to be one in Christ have found that tensions within the church have eternal ramifications and must be handled with care.

Twenty-first century women will live in the context of increasing conflict. Personal, professional, ethnic, and organizational conflict. The call to forgive is constant.

The Woman Who Anointed Jesus' Feet
No one felt the need to have her heart washed clean more than the woman who stood outside the door to the house where Jesus was to dine (See Luke 7:36). She watched as His host, a Pharisee, greeted Him and gave

Him entrance. Others of the uninvited guests joined her just outside the entrance and watched as the official visitors were led to their places at the table. As Jesus and the others reclined at the table, she followed the other intruders to places offering the best vantage points. She chose a place near Jesus, unquestionably the most interesting guest present that night. She clutched the bottle tightly in her hand. She had paid a dear price for its contents, and she would not waste a drop.

Seated behind Jesus, she had easy access to His feet. As she neared him, intending to anoint His feet with the costly ointment, she was overcome by her deep respect for Him. The tears flowed unbidden and fell on His feet. She kissed His feet and wiped her tears away with her hair. The Pharisee host, Simon, was incredulous. "If he were a prophet, he would know who this woman is. Only a prostitute would unloose her hair and touch a man like that." But He said nothing until Jesus broke the silence.

"Simon," He said, "I have something to say to you."

"Teacher, speak."

Jesus told a story about a man who had loaned two men sums of money, one 50 denarii and one 500 denarii. When they were unable to repay the loan, he cancelled the debts.

"Now which of them will love him more?" Jesus asked.

"I suppose the one for whom he cancelled the greater debt," Simon was forced to say.

"You have judged rightly," and then Jesus turned to the woman, praising her for her love poured out on Him. He contrasted her acts of devotion—washing His feet with her tears and drying them with her hair—with Simon's neglect of the customary courtesy of washing

His feet. Nor had Simon anointed His head with oil, but the woman had rubbed His feet with a costly ointment.

"Therefore, Simon, her sins, which were many, have been forgiven; hence she has shown great love."

Then turning to the Pharisee, Jesus said, "But the one to whom little is forgiven, loves little."

Two heard the teaching of Jesus regarding forgiveness that evening. One went away joyful, born anew. Her lilting song might have been:
Happy are those whose transgression is forgiven,
Whose sin is covered (Psalm 32:1).

The second, the Pharisee host, joined his colleagues in complaining: "Who does he think he is—God?"

Forgive and Be Forgiven

Have you ever sung the doxology and every verse of every hymn and quoted the Lord's Prayer in the worship service without being consciously aware of any of it? Instead you mentally reviewed comments from the Sunday School class, checked who was sitting where, and read the announcements in the bulletin. You gave every outward appearance of total involvement in worship, mentally and spiritually. In reality, you had checked out.

When we make that discovery, it's interesting to read the hymns again to see just what we have promised to do. Maybe you have sung "Here I raise mine Ebenezer," and you don't even know what an Ebenezer is! Did we bypass our hearts as well when we joined the congregation reciting the model prayer: "And forgive us our debts as we forgive our debtors"?

With the words of the redeemed through the centuries, we have asked God to forgive us in accordance to our forgiving others. We love to read Paul's words to the Colossians: "And when you were dead in trespasses and the uncircumcision of your flesh, God made you alive together with him, when he forgave us all our trespasses" (Colossians 2:13).

Is our being forgiven by God contingent upon our forgiving persons who have offended us? Jesus said: "For if you forgive others their trespasses, your heavenly Father will also forgive you; but if you do not forgive others, neither will your Father forgive your trespasses" (Matthew 6:14–15).

Pretty straightforward! He loves us and has paid in full for the forgiveness He offers us. It is a priceless gift we freely receive, but there is a price. For Jesus, it was His sacrificial gift of Himself. For us, it is the willingness to forgive others.

In *Why Forgive?*, Johann Christoph Arnold tells of many cases when victims of horrendous crimes or their families find forgiveness of the perpetrators difficult if not impossible. The parents of a brutally murdered child, Jews victimized by the Nazis, and adults still suffering the effects of sexual abuse all struggle to find some meaning, some logic in the injustices in their lives. One mother expressed it well: "What I did find was a big hole in my soul—and nothing to fill it with."

Few of us deal with problems of the magnitude just mentioned. More of us harbor ill will against those that have offended us, misused us, or questioned our honesty or motives. The resulting breach in the fellowship can do irreparable harm among Christians. The longer the perceived injustice festers, the deeper the damage.

Unresolved Anger
Toddlers playing sweetly together are a joy to behold.

They pat each other, relinquish a treasured toy, and laugh together over a joke that only they understand. It doesn't last. One snatches a teddy bear from the other's tight grasp, and World War 3 1/2 breaks out. They cry, pull hair, bite, and pinch. When Mother tries to negotiate a peace settlement, they dissolve in a joint puddle of tears, and each is led to his or her neutral corner.

Little changes as we mature. We still clash with each other, but we discover more acceptable and effective ways to wage war. We find that we can inflict more pain with biting words than biting teeth. Robbing a person of her reputation proves to be far more damaging and enduring than mere snatching of a tangible object. Petty acts of enmity pack more wallop than a literal blow to the head.

The results of our altercations as adults are far more lasting and comprehensive, as well. Unlike children who quickly forget the quarrel, we women often cannot let it go. We roll it around in our minds, remembering each barbed statement, tasting every tear. As a result, dear friendships die, and partnerships are dissolved. Feuding Christians seek supporters and destroy the fellowship within a church. Even strangers are aware of the hostility and continue their search for acceptance elsewhere.

The horrific results of unresolved anger have grown increasingly costly in recent years. Who has not been glued to the television awaiting the full story of yet another school tragedy? Children gather arsenals of weapons and ammunition, usually from their own homes, to kill classmates and teachers for some perceived insult. Mothers hug and kiss their children going off to school. They hope and pray they will arrive home in safety.

What then are the choices we women have when others do us wrong? Or do we have a choice?

Don't Get Mad, Get Even

In advising victims of any wrongdoing, some would say, "Don't get mad. Get even!" This reaction captures and plays off the anger and resentment that gush so naturally out of personal attack. It reflects the Old Testament regulation of "an eye for an eye." According to this law, any Israelite who maimed another should suffer the same injury in return. An eye for an eye, tooth for tooth. You return harm for harm.

In the twenty-first century this is still the chosen response for many. Abused women kill their husbands when they find no other way out, and juries exonerate them. Women kidnap their own children and spirit them away to protect them from mistreatment by their husbands. Fearing a delay in settling scores or dismissal of the charges altogether, a woman may do anything rather than nothing to assure adequate response.

In the Sermon on the Mount, however, Jesus revisited the Leviticus Law. His interpretation was quite different from that followed in the Old Covenant. "You have heard it was said, 'An eye for an eye and a tooth for a tooth. But I say to you, 'Do not resist an evildoer. But if anyone strikes you on the right cheek, turn the other also; and if anyone wants to sue you and take your coat, give your cloak as well; and if anyone forces you to go one mile, go also the second mile. Give to everyone who begs from you, and do not refuse anyone who wants to borrow from you" (Matthew 5:38–42).

In *The Divine Conspiracy: Rediscovering Our Hidden Life in God*, Dallas Willard speaks of "the great inversion" between the human order and the kingdom order.

Within the human order you return harm for harm. But when standing within God's kingdom, "the presumption is precisely reversed." There we will return good for evil, doing more than is strictly required to help others. We do not retaliate when someone hurts us, but willingly accept their abuses. If someone sues me and wins a judgment, I will give him over and above that which the courts have granted. When someone in authority over me orders me to carry his briefcase for one mile, I should willingly continue on with him for another mile. Never, ever, should we refuse to give to one in need or to someone who asks us for something. Astounding! Can anyone honestly comply with this new "inversion?"

Does this passage mean then that a woman caught in an abusive situation should continue to suffer the verbal attacks and physical blows and do nothing? A tactic often used by a man who beats his wife is making her believe she somehow deserves it. Over time she begins to feel that everything is all her fault, and she accepts whatever comes as just punishment. Never in Scripture, however, is a woman told to stay in such a relationship. Instead, extricating herself from the situation is the most redemptive action she can take for both herself and her husband. From this more stable vantage point, a woman can evaluate her past and plan for her future without fear. The space allows both to gain a clearer perspective on themselves and their relationship. Fortunate indeed is the woman who finds a "safe house" or shelter that provides counseling in the midst of such a turbulent time!

While withdrawal from a volatile situation may be wise in any case, many prefer the "eye for an eye" vindication. Squeamish about drawing blood, they shred another's reputation without flinching, not realizing that the weapon is two-edged. It strikes the heart of both victim and perpetrator. Vengeance is never well served in the life of the Christian. Why? Because it is not ours. In Romans, Paul lists the marks of the true Christian. Among other commands, he instructs: "Beloved, never avenge yourselves, but leave room for the wrath of God; for it is written, 'Vengeance is mine, I will repay, says the Lord.' No, 'if your enemies are hungry, feed them; if they are thirsty, give them something to drink; for by doing this you will heap burning coals on their heads.' Do not be overcome by evil, but overcome evil with good" (Romans 12:19–21).

Don't Get Mad, Get Out

When little boys, and big ones, too, "put up their dukes" to resolve a difference, the universal remedy is separation. "Give them time to cool off," we wisely agree. Back off a little and give both parties a chance to recover. We women tend naturally to follow this pattern as we grow up. More often than not we internalize conflict rather than confront someone. You know, it's not "ladylike." Like men, our faces turn red and our blood pressure rises. Fight or flight? We typically choose the latter. Sometimes, avoiding immediate conflict can help matters, giving time for cooling off and prayer. However, too often we never come together to address the conflict. The wound is too deep for a peaceful solution, we think. Better to leave, join another church, whatever it takes to forget the whole thing. Finding new friends, never having to see or interact with the offender, perhaps we can put the offense clear out of our minds. Wrong.

By distancing ourselves from our adversary, we create

distance between our Lord as well. Only by forgiving their "trespasses" can we receive forgiveness for ourselves. If you have ever tried to run from the fallout of a hurt, you know the futility. Bringing your offering, you remember the pointed direction of Jesus: "When you are offering your gift at the altar, if you remember that your brother or sister has something against you, leave your gift there before the altar and go; first be reconciled . . . and then come and offer your gift" (Matthew 5:23–24).

Euodia and Syntyche

I'm sure Euodia and Syntyche didn't want their disagreement to become public—certainly not to be chronicled in the Holy Bible! However, what began as a private tension soon spilled over into the church body. We can almost see it. Some members positioned themselves behind one or the other and expanded the battle. Others, spiritually more mature, grieved that harm was being done to the fellowship and work of the congregation.

Paul, having poured so much energy into the Philippian church, was disappointed that these two courageous women who had struggled beside him in the work of the gospel now struggled against each other. In his letter to the church at Philippi he pleaded with Euodia and Syntyche to be reunited, to be of the same mind. He further requested that a church leader facilitate their reconciliation (Philippians 4:2–3). Why did Paul consider the personal feud between two women to be critical enough to claim his personal intervention? Because tension within the church cripples its work. Because divisions within the body prohibit the effective work of the Spirit within us. Because ill will between members saps the energy and robs us of the joy in service. In another letter Paul addresses the problem again: "Bear with one another and, if anyone has a complaint against another, forgive each other; just as the Lord has forgiven you, so you also must forgive" (Colossians 3:13).

Are Euodia and Syntyche typical in our churches today? Do we women tear down all that the Holy Spirit seeks to build up? Before we are too quick to defend ourselves, we must agree that a germ of truth is contained in that position. However, it could also be said that women are equipped by nature to handle opposition effectively. Because of our God-given impulses toward consensus and relationship, we work patiently toward resolution. We are uncomfortable with controversy and actively seek the healing process. Frustration results when no solution is forthcoming. But time and again I have been encouraged and inspired to see women, in the midst of conflict, keep their eyes focused on a higher goal and fly above the fray. God has invested in women the desire and the gifts to live peaceably with all. Occasionally, however, we have to remind ourselves to: "Put away from you all bitterness and wrath and anger and wrangling and slander, together with all malice, and be kind to one another, tenderhearted, forgiving one another, as God in Christ has forgiven you. Therefore, be imitators of God" (Ephesians 4:31 to 5:1).

CHAPTER 3

Forgiving Yourself

I will change your name;
You shall no longer be called
Wounded, outcast, lonely or afraid.
I will change your name;
Your new name shall be
Confidence, joyfulness
Overcoming one,
Faithfulness, friend of God,
One who seeks my face.
—D. J. Butler

We had just sung the final hymn and heard the benediction. I stepped outside to enjoy the cool New Mexico mountain air for a moment. The missions conference would conclude the next day.

I watched as people fanned out over the grounds. Youth shouted to their friends, hoping to make the most of the last night together. Adults piled in cars and headed for the Chuck Wagon for popcorn, ice cream, and fellowship. Only a small circle of friends remained inside the auditorium. They were discussing with a young man the decision he made at the evening's service.

The annual missions conference was a popular one for people seriously considering a call to missions. An impassioned missionary serving in a distant country had given a powerful message. This year, many responded to the urgent request to help win people to Christ.

Having served as missionaries in Indonesia, my husband Bill and I had a vested interest in this week. He was then on the staff of the mission board's home office and had planned the program for the week. I served as an educational consultant to missionary families, and was meeting with missionary children and their parents during conference days. We both had prayed that new missionaries would respond during the conference, and the Spirit of God had answered in a mighty way.

I wanted to stay and rejoice with this group of friends, but I had scheduled two parent conferences after the service. Reluctantly, I turned to go back inside again.

The first conference was going well. The MK (missionaries' kid) had demonstrated above average achievement for his grade placement, not unusual for these children. Suddenly, we were interrupted by a plaintive cry from the auditorium. We moved to the hall where the little cluster of friends explained the mysterious cry.

The group of friends had been celebrating with the young man his decision to seek appointment as a missionary. None of his friends were surprised; almost anyone who knew him well expected he would be called into a Christian vocation. But when the young man's fiancée realized the impact of his decision, her joy of the moment dissipated. She was ready to gladly join the man she loved in serving her Lord anywhere. She shared his excitement. One fact, however, turned this time of praise into bitter anguish. The mission board had a hard-and-fast rule never to appoint anyone who had been divorced, whatever the cause.

She had been young and impulsive; her first marriage had not been right from the beginning. In the end, her husband found it impossible to maintain the marriage vows, and he chose not to be married to her any longer. The separation and final break had been difficult. She found renewed hope in this man who shared her commitment to Christ. The two of them had discussed ways they could serve the Lord as a couple, but now all this had changed. His decision this evening would preempt any plan for a joint ministry, at least under this mission board. Neither of them had imagined that her past error might stand in the way of their serving together. Her agony, issuing from a broken heart, spilled over in a kind of keening cry. Were her life's plans to serve God with the one she loved to be thwarted by a mistake she had made years ago? It was a moment of unforgettable pathos.

Forgive and Forget?

What woman does not brood over past mistakes that she would like to have expunged from memory? We women are human. Beginning with Eve, the mother of humankind, we've always made mistakes. And we pay for them—sometimes dearly. As Christians we have received God's forgiveness and accepted His promise to remember our sins no more. Unfortunately, we often torture ourselves by reliving the shame and regret. Our inability to forgive ourselves leaves us plagued with guilt and recrimination. "Why did I do it? What weakness made me fall into that trap?" we ask ourselves.

We worry about the confidentiality of others who are aware of our past. Will they betray us by leaking the information? The lurid details are not always necessary. Just the hint of a skeleton in the closet can set tongues wagging, defeat a political candidate, spoil job possibilities, and cripple a Christian witness.

Fortunately, God forgives even the darkest sin if we by faith ask Him. As women of other millennia have discovered, the Faithful One desires to release us from all past sins. Can we let go of our own sense of guilt, self-hate, and recrimination? It is the nature of the beast to revisit the sin; it is the nature of God to forget.

The following stories of three women reveal the burden of past mistakes. Two of them are believers and in many ways have felt the deeper guilt. The third had never heard of a redeeming God and lived the only life she knew. Their stories are true; their names have been changed. Perhaps you or someone you know will identify with one of them and find the release they discovered.

Janet's Story

Janet knew she was in love—not just thought, but knew. Even before his family joined her church, she had noticed him. Too shy to actually talk to him, she merely watched him from a distance. "What a gorgeous man!" she thought, "and he sings, too!" Though hardly a man at sixteen, Jim turned the heads of other girls, too. Janet, a beautiful teenager, tentatively made the first move. Her high school sorority dance was to be held in April, and she decided to ask Jim. But she, like other girls of the '60s, was unaccustomed to asking guys out. How would she find courage to issue the invitation? She had her opportunity after a youth handbell practice at the church. Forgetting her practiced speech, she blurted out her question. When he said "yes," she was ecstatic. Her family still teases her these many years later about relaying the experience perched atop the refrigerator. "But, hey, when I look back on it, it was one of those days when things were never going to be the same."

Jim graduated and attended a fine university in the

city where they lived. A year later Janet enrolled in a university in a nearby city. She spent her weekends at home to be near Jim. As time passed their intimacy grew, and in December she was pregnant. She kept her secret even from Jim until March, when he insisted she go to the infirmary.

"Do you know you're pregnant?" asked the attending physician.

Know? How could she not know? She even wondered how she had been able to sleep with this baby kicking inside her—all in a dormitory among girls who had no inkling of her situation.

Janet felt an urgency to complete the school year; her college career was in jeopardy. Because of the Kent State University tragedy, Janet's university allowed students with an A average to opt out of final exams, in an attempt to deter any uprisings on their campus. So Janet, five-and-a-half months pregnant, went home. Jim presented her with a diamond engagement ring, and what was a joyful time for her parents brought renewed feelings of failure and guilt. Above all she hated deceiving her parents.

But her mother intuitively knew. As she and her parents discussed the dilemma, tears flowed. "I did not understand what those tears were really about. Later I realized that my parents' tears were not shed in condemnation. What I did know was that I had not conformed to standard and there would be consequences to pay. But not to them." They were disappointed and sad, but they loved her no less. Janet says, "I can only hope my eyes and hands have conveyed that same unconditional love to my own children."

Her parents went immediately to their closest friends to share the news. In the years that followed their support has never wavered. What could have marked a tragedy has become instead a part of Janet and Jim's Christian journey.

"We were young parents; you might say we all grew up together. Loren has been such a blessing in our lives. What a loss it would have been not to have this precious one! How could God have blessed us so after what we did?" How, indeed? God's grace, His unmerited favor. What Christian has not needed—and received—His forgiveness and love?

"How long did it take for you to forgive yourself, Janet?" I quietly probed.

With great anguish she threw up her hands, "Oh, twenty years!" Forgiving oneself—ah! that is a different story. Today Janet and Jim have seen all their children grow up and leave home. They have successful careers and respected places in the community. Those who were in the church when Loren was born have all but forgotten the details. They only know the Janet and Jim of today, an attractive committed couple who teach a Sunday School class of young married couples, sing in the choir, and go on a missions trip together each year.

Catherine's Story
Catherine drove into her driveway, stopping long enough to get the day's mail. As she juggled packages from the morning's Christmas shopping, she thought nothing would be better than a cup of soup to soothe her weary bones. Putting the bowl into the microwave, she sat down to review the mail. A large packet fell out from among the collection of Christmas cards, bills, and third-class mail. Catherine was surprised to see that it was from her daughter. "Why is she sending me a package so close to the time when she will be coming home

from the university for the holidays?" she mused.

Rescuing her bowl of soup from the microwave, she sat down to feast on her lunch and the contents of the package. As she opened it, three books and a fat letter fell out. As she read the book titles, she realized they were about homosexuality. Her heart sank. Could her daughter be a lesbian?

Putting the books aside, Catherine opened the folded papers and began to read the dreaded story. Her daughter confessed her love for a young woman with whom she had been living for over a year. She then told how they planned to make their union public through a commitment service when she was graduated. When Catherine had finished reading the large sheaf of papers, she had already begun to compose in her mind what she knew would be the hardest letter she had ever written. It began:

Dear Angela,
When I read your letter, I thought I was reading my own autobiography. I understood and identified with everything you wrote except the public exposure and acceptance parts.

Catherine stopped to renew her resolve. She had prayed that she would never have to open her past secret to public review, but she had told the Lord that she was willing to share the experiences if she needed to. And if there was ever a time she needed to, this was it. What followed was a frank and personal letter about Catherine's own struggles with homosexuality.

As she faced the difficult task, memories of years she wanted to forget flooded Catherine's mind. She and her twin sister had been born fifty years before into a strong Christian family that cheerfully attended their local church every time the doors were open. Although physically identical, she and her sister were as different as daylight and dark. Catherine was a tomboy, choosing to ride bikes and play cowboys and Indians, marbles, and all kind of ball games. Her sister preferred dolls and playing "house." Catherine always wanted to be a boy and was told frequently by her mother that she was the boy they never had. She chafed at having to wear dresses to school, when she much preferred jeans!

Catherine never felt close to her mother, even having ambivalent feelings toward her. She disliked her critical spirit but admitted she was a "good mother," an effective disciplinarian. Catherine and her sister were excellent and well-behaved students. They had to be; it was required!

"I remember my first crush in the eighth or ninth grade on the star of the girls' basketball team," she continued to write. "But I just repressed it—put it away." In high school she herself was the star basketball player and valedictorian, while her twin was salutatorian. They were model children. While Catherine often experienced great feelings of anger toward her parents, she was not allowed to express them, and therefore never learned to have open, honest communication, even with her sister.

During college, she spent her summers working in church camps. At the university she became involved in ministry to internationals, a work that captured her heart. Upon graduation, she was accepted as a two-year missionary to Africa. During that time she experienced born-again salvation and a strengthening of her relationship with God. In spite of her commitment to God, however, she occasionally struggled with homosexual thoughts and feelings in her teaching assignment at a

Baptist girl's high school in Nigeria. She continued to correspond with a young man in the States, a student at the Air Force Academy. When he proposed, she said yes. He was the Christian man of her dreams, someone who could bring her closeness and comfort.

One month after Catherine arrived in North Carolina, she married Ron. It was too soon; she had had no time to adjust to her re-entry into American culture after her two years in Africa. To make matters worse, they returned from their honeymoon to discover that Ron was to report for an assignment to Vietnam. Catherine was wrestling with severe emotional and spiritual problems, but the six weeks of training before Ron left for Vietnam did not seem to be the time to deal with them.

The year they were separated, Catherine worked in church camps and with internationals. She met Ron for R & R in Hawaii, but she felt strange and somehow detached from him. Back in North Carolina she continued to struggle with homosexual desires.

When Ron returned he was assigned to Fort Walton Beach, Florida. Once again Catherine got involved in the church's international ministry and was soon directing the program. The civil war in Nigeria was over, and she began to correspond with a former student who had shown great academic potential. When she and Ron issued the young girl an invitation to come to the US to attend college, she quickly accepted their proposal to live with them for her stay.

Catherine and the Nigerian student began to spend much time together, and soon strong sexual feelings evolved into consensual sexual relations. The months that followed were a windstorm of conflicted feelings, enjoyment of a forbidden relationship, and counter feelings of shame and self-hate. She became an atheist and contemplated suicide. The guilt she experienced was excruciating.

"I finally became so sick of myself that I was able to break it off," she told her daughter. She fell on her knees and repented.

Catherine continued to pour out her heart to her daughter in the letter. She related other liaisons with women through the years. The war within herself reflected the conflict of homosexual desires and yearnings for Christ's presence in her life. Years of agony spilled out over the stationery before her. She included pages of Bible verses that had bolstered her own faith, hoping they would provide Angela with the same spiritual strength.

She concluded her letter with, "It has been very difficult but freeing for me to write all this. As you can see, I will be able to understand you and what you are going through. As much as I love you, God loves you even more."

After Catherine sealed the letter to Angela, she realized she had to share it all with Ron. He was an airline pilot and was away at the time. When he returned, she gave both letters to him and left him alone to read them. After some time, he came to her, took her in his arms, and held her for a long time. This godly man loved and forgave. Their marriage grows ever stronger. Their union today is based on faith in each other and in the God they serve together. She made a confession before the church she grew up in and to the church in which she was then a member, attempting to be faithful to the spirit of Proverbs 28:13: "He who conceals his sins does not prosper, but whoever confesses and renounces them finds mercy" (NIV). Following one such confession, the pastor wrote in the church paper: "The testimony shared recently in our church by Catherine was a dynamic demonstration of the power of testimony, of the joy of spiritual victory, of the strength that comes from others who can share our griefs and joys. It reminded us all that God changes lives, that He heals and restores. And what encouragement it gives to others who struggle!"

In the months that followed, Catherine began an in-depth study of the Bible. Formerly, she had relied on Christian biographies and books about the Bible. Now she found the truth of Hebrews 4:12: "The word of God is living and active. Sharper than any double-edged sword, it penetrates even to dividing soul and spirit, joints and marrow; it judges the thoughts and attitudes of the heart" (NIV).

She experienced a hunger for the Truth she had never known before, and reveled in the beauty and mystery and relevance of God's Word. "I've made my choice to be heterosexual—to be the woman and wife God made me to be. God will empower me to live up to this commitment as long as I abide in Him and His Word abides in me" (John 15:7).

Catherine attends an ex-gay support group, and she and Ron lead a Parents and Friends of Ex-Gays group. It meets monthly to provide support for family and friends who love and care for someone who struggles with same-sex attraction, but who view homosexual behavior as sinful. "It has been helpful to me to realize that one definition of sin is 'missing the mark' or the 'target' God has planned for a person's life. God's target for me is acceptance of my God-given femininity and heterosexuality. I praise the Lord that He gave me the courage to risk the journey of opening my life to others.

This exciting journey of a lifetime has only begun. God is awesome!"

Karen's Story

Unlike Janet and Catherine, Karen never knew what it was like to grow up in a Christian home or to be exposed to Christian influences. She experienced life instead in a very dysfunctional family comprised of her mother, a single parent on disability for a neck injury, and three older siblings. Her mother and a constant swarm of friends taught her that life was cheap and that alcohol, if you drank enough of it, brought relief. Her sisters and brother were absorbed in their own lives, "so I pretty much grew up on my own—and fast," Karen acknowledges. She began to drink and skip school at fifteen.

"I started sleeping around at sixteen. It made me feel wanted and needed, and for the first time in my life, I was in control." Karen's natural beauty and tendency to look older than her age assured an abundance of suitors. Even the older troublemakers began to hang around, elevating the excitement of her life in the fast lane.

She soon discovered there was a toll to be paid for the lifestyle she had chosen. Her friends began dropping like flies, victims of car accidents and suicide. Discovering by accident the identity of her biological father was a major blow, made worse because she knew him and saw him almost every day. "What a fool I was!" she thought. "Why didn't someone tell me?"

Karen finished high school but was denied her diploma because of her many absences. Instead of making the deficiencies up in summer school, she moved with her mother to Kissimmee, Florida. She began barhopping and moving in and out of relationships with men. In the midst of it all, she started using heroin, causing her to lose her job as waitress—the only means she had of supporting her $500 a day drug habit. Even the meager amount she earned from a similar job would never sustain her added addiction to cocaine. Only one recourse was available to her—prostitution. She entered into it reluctantly as a means for satisfying a growing need for drugs. She did find it to have one benefit—a sense of belonging, of being a part. Like many others, as her drug dependency increased, conversely her sense of caring about anybody or anything decreased. She found jail a peaceful respite from her life in the streets, offering good food and a warm bed.

On the streets, however, she was consumed with rage toward those who seemed to have it all together. Her loneliness was as interminable as her craving for drugs. The drugs and loneliness fed each other. All the correctional officers knew her by name during the eight years of her intermittent incarceration.

One fateful day when Karen was in jail, she was told she had a visitor. Looking through the glass, she was pleased to see it was a man she knew from the streets. He seemed different though, so—peaceful! He seemed to have changed in the way she wished she could, but what was it? He shared an unbelievable story of deliverance and forgiveness that has changed countless lives over time. He had found hope for the future. Because she had been kind to him on the streets, he wanted to share Jesus with her.

Karen could not understand the feeling she experienced, but she wanted it never to stop. No one had ever told her about this gentle Savior who loved her. New knowledge of Him made her yearn for more. She wanted to know everything! She longed to experience the peace and joy that radiated from her friend. He visited her faithfully to share Jesus and His love for all humankind. As she began to understand and believe, she gave her heart to this forgiving Savior and committed her life to Him. Never in her life had she believed in anything. Now she was on fire for the Lord.

"Karen, I want to introduce a Christian woman, a friend in my church, to you," he said. "She has much to teach you in your new walk."

Everything within her shouted, "No!" Shame and guilt filled her heart. She could not bear to have it exposed to another. She trusted her friend, but what he was asking seemed too difficult. When the visitor arrived, however, Karen was surprised to see that she had tattoos and was casually dressed. It was obvious when the woman began to speak that she had experienced the kind of life Karen knew. Their conversations that followed in the weeks to come built on that initial bonding. Her new friend shared a vision of starting a ministry for women coming out of jail, and she wanted Karen to be involved.

When Karen was released from jail, her friend picked her up. She moved to Orlando to help begin Restoration Ministries for Women. "The best decision I have ever made was to give my life to the Lord. Now my life has purpose, and I have finally found true peace and joy through our Lord Jesus Christ. My calling is to share with the churches the struggles and despair that women out there go through. Also, to share with the women out there the hope found in Jesus Christ."

Cast the First Stone
Karen, if she had grown up in Judea two millennia ago, would probably have been condemned to die because of

her promiscuous life. John's Gospel in chapter eight tells of a woman who was dragged to Jesus by a spiteful, angry mob. "Teacher, this woman was caught in the very act of committing adultery. In the Law, Moses commanded us to stone such a woman. What do you say?" they asked.

The mob was made up of teachers of the Law and Pharisees. They were not so much indignant about the woman's sins as they were eager to fault Jesus. Faithful Jews were following Him wherever He led. The current rumor mill was alive with stories of His claims to forgive sins and to offer Living Water, whatever that was! Fearful of totally losing control of the masses to this self-proclaimed teacher, they came to put an end to His boasts by exposing Him before many of His followers.

They thought they had Him with this question! Had there been a first-century "high five," they would certainly have been inclined to use it. But just as they lifted their palms, Jesus bent down and began to write with His finger on the ground. The irate crowd assaulted Him with questions, growing angrier at His continued silence. Finally, Jesus stood and quietly said, "Let anyone among you who is without sin be the first to throw a stone at her."

That certainly shut the mouths of Jesus' questioners. If a sinless person lived somewhere in Jerusalem, the scribes and Pharisees did not know, but they knew one thing—he was not in the crowd that day. As Jesus bent down again, the crowd dispersed until only Jesus and the woman were left. Standing up, Jesus asked, "Woman, where are they? Has no one condemned you?"

No one, sir." She stood before him incredulous.

"Neither do I condemn you. Go your way, and from now on do not sin again." Just as Jesus worked with miraculous, forgiving power in the life of this first-century Jewish woman, so He redeemed Karen in the twentieth century.

Karen grew up never hearing the message of Christ. No one from a church visited her home; she never had a mentor to help her through the teen years. The good news of Jesus was as remote to her as any unreached person in the world. Just like Karen, women live in your city or town, perhaps in the shadow of your church, who have never heard the story of Jesus' forgiving love. They need someone to share the gospel with them. Could it be you?

Ministries with the homeless, the poor, and the illiterate provide opportunities for modeling God's love. A worker in a women's shelter told me recently about Alice, a long-time resident of the shelter. No one had ever seen her when she was not drunk, but one day a volunteer left a sewing machine, and Alice began sewing. Another volunteer came and taught her how to quilt; soon she presented the shelter with a prize-worthy quilt—and another and another. Now Alice is teaching quilting in a large university in the city, and no one can remember the last time she was drunk. Today she has eternal hope and purpose as well, because a volunteer, a woman, came.

Alice, Janet, Catherine, and Karen are survivors, even overcomers of their past. They have moved beyond the paralysis of guilt and are involved in ministries to others who, like themselves, need someone to walk beside them. As Karen observed, her mentor had been where she was. While her male friend led her to the Lord, she needed a woman to mentor her.

Janet, with her husband, nurtures young married couples in Sunday School. No one could do it better.

She knows first-hand the value of a strong, nurturing family that holds fast in times of trouble. Every week she emails the women in their class to encourage and challenge them in their Christian walk. What an example she is to those young wives! Catherine and Karen have become rescuers, reaching out to women who desperately need a second, and often a third hand up.

Janet and Catherine were reared in a Christian home, with families that faithfully attended church. Neither of these important factors, however, could guarantee a life free from mistakes. Who failed them? How could they have avoided the mistakes of the past? Surely we women of the church must bear some responsibility of our own.

The Work of the Church Inside and Out

In 1993, LifeWay Christian Resources launched a unique program for youth. True Love Waits challenges youth to remain sexually abstinent until marriage. You may remember seeing thousands of commitment cards posted on convention center lawns, churches, and even on the Mall in Washington, D.C.

In the intervening years many have wondered about the effectiveness of such a vow. Are teenagers who sign such a pledge more resistant to the pressures and temptations in this permissive society than those who do not? In the teenage years, when hormones are raging, and when TV, movies, and books urge youth toward sex, is it realistic to think that a commitment made for sexual purity could make a difference?

A study entitled, "Promising the Future: Virginity Pledges as They Affect the Transition to First Intercourse" found that "teenagers who pledge to remain sexually abstinent until marriage are 34 percent less likely to have sex than those who do not take virginity vows. . . . Pledging decreases the risk of intercourse outside of marriage substantially and independently." One of the researchers stated that virginity pledges give teens a way to say no. The result of such emphases as True Love Waits is that fewer teens experience unwanted pregnancies and sexually transmitted diseases. Those who had previously been sexually active but signed the pledge to remain abstinent "from this day forward" were liberated from practices that had held them in bondage.

Churches are generally reluctant to sponsor programs related to sex. We are afraid the leaders will not handle the topic properly, and "things might get out of hand." Anxious lest the church be accused of treading on "parental ground," we choose to avoid risky topics altogether. The schools typically give good instruction related to *facts* through the sex education program, but they are not permitted to address the *values* related to it. Parents are often too busy or too embarrassed to keep open dialogue with their teenager. As a result, the only input the teenager gets is from a friend or acquaintance who is never too busy or embarrassed or fearful to pass on their experiences and incomplete knowledge. Do we really want to empower an immature, unbridled, non-Christian high school teenager with sole access to our treasured youth?

Stop, stop, you are saying. Our church must be the exception, because we have not forfeited our responsibility in this area. Hurray! Many churches have met this need with special seminars and retreats. Normally, parents are informed prior to the meeting and do not hear of the purpose after the fact. Youth ministers and leaders divide the boys and girls, placing women with the girls and men with the boys. If you have served in this capacity, you know the youth are eager to discuss the topic. For the most part, they deal with it in a mature way. The most valuable outcome of the effort is the open door it creates for future conversations. Frank discussions of homosexuality, drugs, abortion, and other controversial topics may follow in a safe and appropriate setting.

Forgiveness in the Church

And Catherine? How could the church have intervened in her pull toward homosexuality? So much has been aired on TV and radio, written in newspapers and magazines, that Christians fear even saying the word within the walls of the church building.

Some years ago, church members were paralyzed by fear in another crisis. Knowing little about the cause and effects of AIDS, we church members put our heads in the sand, praying, "Dear God, please let it go away." We hoped no one stricken by that condition would come to church. When they did, fear trumped compassion, and many AIDS patients and/or their families suffered yet another rejection. Today, wise church leaders have developed policies to assure safety for babies in the nursery and support groups to offer assistance to AIDS patients. We have better understanding of the condition and realize the opportunity for ministry and evangelism it brings. Perhaps women will lead out in providing equally effective programs for those struggling with homosexuality.

Catherine reported now being active in a support group for families of people living the homosexual lifestyle. Would your church be open to host such an organization knowing it might invite strong criticism, both outside and inside the membership? But if not the church, then who? We have played it safe too long; perhaps now is the time for risking in Christ's name. His openness to sinners is our example. Do we dare?

We women too often fear contamination, criticism, and reputation more than we fear hearing our Lord's condemnation, "I was hungry, thirsty, a stranger, naked, sick, in prison and you did not care for me." In challenging times, controversial times, we are too often disengaged. From the sowing of the whirlwind we have reaped a balmy breeze, where our membership is comforted and warmed by the perennial vacation. AWOL, absent without leave. The early church was a revolutionary body; can we be less?

Women with the heart of God can make the difference for those who need a loving touch. Jesus saved His most caustic rebukes for the pious religious leaders, His most inviting welcome for sinners. God forgive us when trying to emulate Him we get the two mixed up.

Neither Do I Condemn You

Perhaps premarital sex, homosexuality, drug addiction, prostitution, or incarceration are not among your past regrets. You may be wrestling with another indiscretion instead. It is estimated that each year in the US approximately 1.6 million babies are aborted. How many of those babies' mothers were Christian women and now deal with tremendous guilt years after the fact? An arrest for drunk driving, shoplifting, or some other offense for so long kept secret continues to fester within the heart, rendering some of us ineffective in our spiritual growth. Cheating on tax or expense forms, an indiscriminate sexual encounter, a lie that resulted in unexpected outcomes—any action in the past can steal into one's private thoughts and create a spirit of anger, remorse, and self-hate.

Even now the forgiving God is waiting for our confessions; He longs to pour out His loving forgiveness if we will open our hearts to Him. When Jesus defended the adulterous woman in the story reviewed above, He amazed her by saying, "Neither do I condemn you." Many youth and adults long to hear these words of reconciliation. Knowing the release it brings, we women can lead others to know a deeper life in Him. Many are desperately seeking a safe place to share their burdens, confess their sins, and find support. Could you and your church provide such a safe haven?

"Happy are those whose transgression is forgiven" (Psalm 32:1). Immediately after Jesus told the woman that He did not condemn her, He added, "Go your way, and from now on do not sin again." Don't waste your energy regretting a past that has been forgiven; instead give yourself to living the Christ-filled life, full of hope, promise, and victory for you—and for others.

CHAPTER 4

Willing to Risk

Do you remember your first day of school? It may have been a very long time ago, too long to remember precisely what your feelings were, but for many of us it was traumatic. Some of us cried, some refused to budge from the car. Others marched in confidently and made friends quickly.

As difficult as that first time was, we discovered that life is defined by entering new, ever more distant arenas. We choose some destinations; others are selected for us. Successful entries build up confidence for tomorrow's exploration; failures diminish our self-assurance. Many lack the heart for adventure and perhaps settle too soon for comfort and security. Others constantly seek challenges and never "settle down."

What about today's Christian woman? Is it possible, necessary, or forbidden to seek a life of ease and simplicity? Or must we involve ourselves in matters that always keep us a little off-center in order to make a difference in our world? As always, we can learn from past experiences. Consider these women who have willingly risked all for a cherished cause.

Deborah: Judge Turned Warrior

Some women have deliberately chosen dangerous leadership roles, while others have had it thrust upon them. Deborah, charismatic leader of ancient Israel, was one of the latter. Her story is told in the biblical book of Judges. The very fact that she was chosen a judge tells us of the high regard in which she was held; few women wore the mantle of justice in those days. She no doubt exercised her power prudently, making wise and fair decisions. She heard cases not in a courtroom but under a palm tree in the hill country of Ephraim.

Countless times God warned His people by means of the prophets to guard the sanctity of their relationship with Him. Living side by side with Canaanites, Hittites, and other pagan tribes, they were intrigued by their idols and strange elements of worship. From the opening of their minds and hearts it was a short walk to the embracing of the worship of Baal and the Ashtoreths. Intermarriage with the Canaanites and others further knit the two together, an alliance expressly forbidden by God. Blatantly disregarding God's warnings, the Israelites were headed for disaster.

But God would not give them up. His investment in these Israelites was too great to lose them now. He would use a surprising instrument to carry out His plan: King Jabin of Canaan—the enemy! With Sisera, Canaan's powerful and successful general, and his huge arsenal he commanded a formidable force. For twenty years they aimed nine hundred chariots at the defenseless Israelites, destroying the new vineyards, violating their women, and killing their children.

Seated at her arbor bench day after day, year after year, Deborah heard cases of Israelite war victims. She became increasingly indignant at the lack of initiatives in effectively confronting the enemy. When God entrusted her with a strategy to defeat the Canaanites, she called on Barak to discuss the implementation of the plan. This tribal leader, known for his military prowess, hurried to Ephraim to hear Deborah's counsel. The line of attack would be carried out by an army of ten thousand soldiers, which Barak was to muster. They would take their position on Mount Tabor. Meanwhile,

Deborah would draw Sisera, the general, out to a specified area where Barak could easily defeat him.

After thinking over the plan, Barak still hesitated. Finally, he said, "If you go with me, I will go; but if you will not go with me, I will not go" (Judges 4:8). Why did Barak vacillate in accepting the full responsibility that was his and base his decision upon Deborah's willingness to accompany him? He must have seen in her the very presence of God. He would be a fool to go without this power, he reasoned.

"I will surely go with you," she said. "Nevertheless, the road on which you are going will not lead to your glory, for the Lord will sell Sisera into the hand of a woman."

Deborah and Barak set about to form and train the army of ten thousand who gave allegiance to their joint leaders. After all were prepared, the day of action came. "Up! For this is the day on which the Lord has given Sisera into your hand. The Lord is indeed going out before you." As promised, God caused disarray among the Canaanite army, and all the enemy soldiers were killed, but Sisera got out of his chariot and fled on foot.

Sisera escaped to the tent belonging to members of a clan friendly to Canaan, where he felt safe. Jael, the lady of the tent, met him and said, "Turn aside, my lord, turn aside to me; have no fear." After serving the weary general a glass of milk and preparing him a place to rest, she stood at the entrance of the tent. She watched until he fell asleep, and then she quietly took a tent peg and a hammer and drove the peg into the ground— through his temples! Deborah's prophecy was true: "The Lord will sell Sisera into the hand of a woman." Willing to assume new and difficult roles, the two women won rest from war for forty years.

Stand up and Be Counted

In 1995, our nation celebrated the seventy-fifth anniversary of the ratification of the Nineteenth Amendment. It had taken almost as many years for suffragists to achieve the woman's right to vote, and many who had worked so diligently to obtain their goal did not live to see its passing.

Today we women tend to forget that the right to vote is a precious treasure, earned by the daring work of courageous and single-minded women. Many had hoped that after the Civil War was over, women would be given the right to vote, but it was not to be. Although the Fifteenth Amendment gave voting rights to black men in 1870, the women's vote would have to wait fifty more years.

While many attempts were made in the eastern US to break through the impasse, progress in the western areas of the US occurred much more quickly. In 1869 Wyoming led the nation in adopting woman suffrage when it was still a territory. When the US Congress would not approve its statehood in 1890 if it continued to let women vote, Wyoming declared, "We will remain out of the Union a hundred years rather than come in without the women." Utah, Colorado, and Idaho joined their sister states in adopting enfranchisement for women in the 1880s. Five other western states registered women voters between 1910–1912.

In the 1890s, separate groups established for varying purposes set aside their own agenda in order to put their collective weight on the suffrage movement. The Woman's Christian Temperance Union legitimized their involvement by endorsing it as a way of protecting the home, women, and children. Women temporarily withdrew from the race issue, which was still a divisive concern in any forum, to seek voting rights for all women. Black women insisted that if white women needed the vote to protect their rights, then black women—victims of racism as well as sexism—needed the ballot even more.

In the first part of the twentieth century a massive rebuilding program garnered growth from every corner. The socially prominent, new college graduates, followers of the Progressive Movement, civic club members, reformers, labor leaders—all were targeted for membership in the movement. Open-air meetings, parades, and literature distribution fanned the flames. When the US entered World War I, suffragists were urged to postpone their drive for voting rights temporarily in order to support the war effort. By their willingness they won much goodwill from the general public, decision-makers, and especially President Woodrow Wilson. After the war a few more states signed on, and President Wilson led Congress to approve the Nineteenth Amendment and to submit it to the states in June 1919.

Thirty-six states had to ratify the amendment to make it a law. Strange as it may seem, women were among the strongest opponents of women's suffrage. "They truly believed that female involvement in a man's world of politics would damage the family," wrote Ruth A. Tucker, in *Women in the Maze: Questions and Answers on Biblical Equality*. The editor of the Missouri Synod *Witness* reinforced their concern: "Many women will be so busy about voting and political office that the home and children will have no attraction for them, and American mothers and children, like Christian charity, will be a rarity."

By the summer of 1920, only one more state was needed to give women the right to vote, but time was running out. No further legislative sessions were scheduled before the November election. Desperate suffragists were unwilling to concede. They were so close! Remembering the president's gratitude for their assistance in the war effort, they appealed to him to pressure the governor of Tennessee into calling a session.

Suffragists and anti-suffragists descended upon Nashville. It was a cliffhanger, and in the end one vote made the difference. Tennessee reaffirmed its vote for ratification, and the Nineteenth Amendment was officially added to the US Constitution on August 26, 1920. After more than half a century of undying purpose, the women of the US, sublimating their differences, jointly prevailed in their search for the right to vote. These risk-takers defied all opposition to obtain their goal. When you go to your polling site next time, remember the suffragists who risked much in securing your right to stand up and be counted.

Rosa Parks: A Time to Sit
On December 1, 1955, after working all day as a seamstress, Rosa Parks climbed on a bus, paid her fare, and sat down in the last row of the white section of the bus. The law allowed black people to sit in the white section as long as no white person was standing, but if the section became full, the black passengers must move to the back—the entire row would be cleared for one white passenger.

As the front of the bus slowly filled, Rosa rested in her seat. When the driver demanded that her row be cleared for a white passenger, Rosa moved her legs to allow the other three black passengers to vacate their seats. But she did not move. Tired from her day's work, but even more tired of the treatment she and other

African Americans received every day of their lives, she refused to give up her seat. It was not an impulsive decision; Rosa had been thinking about it for months. On this day, she knew she was ready.

That simple act of defiance set off the modern civil rights movement in the US. Rosa Parks became a symbol of strength in the midst of struggle, assurance in a time of uncertainty. She was arrested, tried, and fined for disregarding a city ordinance, but her act triggered a bus boycott that lasted for 381 days. In 1956, the Supreme Court ruled that segregation on public transportation is unconstitutional.

Today we applaud Rosa Parks' bravery in breaking an unjust city ordinance. We, as a nation, look back to those days of African American oppression with shame. We grieve over the injustices they endured. In her childhood Rosa had often covered her ears when she heard the Ku Klux Klan ride at night. Would there be a burning cross in their yard? Or were the hooded men bent on lynching that night? Fear was never far away.

But when the time came, Rosa's action was calculated and fearless. Reflecting on that event almost forty years later, Mrs. Parks writes in her book, *Quiet Strength*, "I kept thinking about my mother and my grandparents, and how strong they were. I knew there was a possibility of being mistreated, but an opportunity was being given to me to do what I had asked of others."

What gave Rosa Parks the courage to take such a stand? Throughout her book she speaks of her belief in God and the centrality of her Christian convictions in everything she does. She writes, "I'd like for [readers] to know that I had a very spiritual background and that I believe in church and my faith and that has helped to give me the strength and courage to live as I did."

Really MADD

Most of us know of someone who has been tragically injured or killed by a drunk driver, but two women did something about it. In 1979 in Maryland, Cindi Lamb and Laura, her five-and-a-half-year-old daughter, were hit head-on by a repeat drunk driver traveling 120 miles per hour. As a result of the crash, Laura became one of the world's youngest quadriplegics. Less than a year later a drunk driver in California killed thirteen-year-old Cari Lightner. Although convicted for drunk driving multiple times, the driver was carrying a valid California license. Fueled by grief and the futility of her daughter's death, Candace Lightner gathered with friends at a steak house in Sacramento and discussed forming Mothers Against Drunk Drivers—or MADD.

Lamb in Maryland and Lightner in California held hands across America, and by 1982 MADD had eleven chapters in four states. As the organization grew, MADD began to receive donations from victims and concerned citizens, and the movement spread to Canada, England, New Zealand, Australia, Guam, and Puerto Rico. Today it is the largest crime victims assistance organization in the world.

MADD originally stood for Mothers Against Drunk Drivers, and its purpose was to mobilize victims and their allies to influence others to see drunk driving as unacceptable, even criminal, and to influence public policy and programs in that regard. In 1984, MADD changed its name to Mothers Against Drunk Driving to focus its energies on fighting drunk driving and supporting victims of this violent crime.

In 2000, MADD updated its mission statement to reflect its efforts to prevent underage drinking, and for good reason. In 1997, 21 percent of the youth involved in fatal crashes had been drinking. Today alcohol is the number one drug among young people. According to MADD statistics, "youth who drink alcohol are 7.5 times more likely to use any illicit drug, and 50 times more likely to use cocaine than young people who never drink alcohol."

How many parents have grieved over the senseless deaths of children at the hands of drunk drivers, but have not known how to turn their tears of grief into tools of action? Lightner and Lamb dared to use the impetus of their loss to strike a deathblow to drunk driving, and we are the beneficiaries of their courage.

Celebrating twenty years of existence, MADD now claims 3 million members and supporters. The organization has achieved amazing results in its lifetime, including:

• Alcohol-related traffic fatalities have declined 43 percent

• More than 138,000 people are alive today because of its efforts

• Untold numbers have received comfort, support and assistance in dealing with the aftermath of a drunk driving crash.

While some risk to preserve the good things in life, others risk to obtain them. Sherri Booz is one of the latter.

A Time to Stand and Wait

Sherri and her husband, Ben, live and work in Hong Kong. As Americans living abroad they are thankful for good friends, significant work, and a loving relationship. But they lacked one thing—a child of their own. After endless tests, the doctors feared that Sherri would never conceive except through medical intervention.

In the fall of 1996 she and Ben began to inquire among their friends in various corners of the world about the possibilities for adoption in their countries. Various leads resulted in dead ends, and Sherri became very discouraged. Too often that disappointment took the form of anger vented toward Ben. He seemed to be able to get on with life, while Sherri's heart was broken.

In January 1998, Sherri and Ben went to Nepal to investigate adoptions. For the first time in many months they were encouraged, even when warned that it would probably be twelve to eighteen months before they could expect to hear anything. Sherri prayed on leaving the airport, "Lord, next time we leave this airport, please let our child be with us."

On Valentine's night, 1998, Sherri again poured out her heart to God, once again affirming her trust and acceptance of His timeline. Then, for the first time, she felt God say, "Your baby is being created, even as you give thanks. If your child were already born, you would not be privileged to pray for his or her growth and development in the mother's womb." After crying out her gratitude, Sherri ran to the book she had brought from the US for just this time. The descriptions and photographs of a baby's development week by week in the uterus caused her heart to quicken. She followed the progression from the time of inception, the first beating of the heart, and the appearance of little nubs that grew to be arms and legs.

The agony Sherri had experienced for so long disappeared. In its place came a contentment she had missed. The book that she had planned to use when she herself became pregnant was never far away. Now she prayed for her child being nurtured in another's womb. Two weeks later she felt God say that the baby would be born in May. Sure enough, in May she received an email stating that a baby girl had been born that they should consider. In a follow-up telephone call Sherri and Ben learned that the baby's mother had died during childbirth and that the father had three living children and could not afford another. In addition they were told that the adoption process should proceed without a hitch, because every requirement of Nepalese law was met. It sounded too good to be true.

Sherri arrived in Kathmandu after a long flight and was taken to her friend's home where she would meet her baby for the first time. Sherri wrote, "I saw our daughter lying in her crib. She was so tiny, and her dark brown skin was so beautiful against the white sheet. My heart began to pound out of my chest. With my hands shaking, I picked up all six pounds of her for the first time. My heart was full."

Weeks later in Nepal, Sherri faced one final step of the adoption. The law required that they obtain the signature of the local government official of the baby's birth family. To do this, she had to go personally to the father's village some distance away from Kathmandu. Sherri knew the trek would be difficult. Ben had an assignment that could not be delayed, and she would have to manage without him. They were to go by truck as far as possible to meet the birth father and guide for the final leg of the journey. She dreaded the trip—six hours on foot. Abby ("giver of joy") Elizabeth ("dedicated") was nestled against her snugly. Sherrie, the assistant to the attorney, the birth father, and the guide set out.

Sherri fussed over her baby. It was such a long trip. "Please, God, help her weather this part of the journey." She had a list of the many necessities: special formula for the baby and water to make it, and food for herself. "Food for me!" she thought. "Where is it?" A quick search yielded nothing, and then she remembered having seen it in the kitchen. She must have forgotten to pick it up at the last minute. Well, she would just not eat until they got back. Who would care for Abby if she should become ill by eating unsafe food?

The trail was not a Himalayan climb, but it was not a simple, flat walk either. Little Abby and the necessities Sherri brought along for her care became increasingly heavy. Finally, after six-and-a-half hours, they arrived in the village. Sherri was amazed to find Coca-Colas at the little store—hot, but wet anyway. She was dismayed, however, when she was told that the papers could not be signed until the next day. She prayed that she had enough water for Abby's formula.

Sherri spent a miserable evening. No electricity, no lights, but a plentiful supply of heat, mosquitoes, and curious villagers. She spent the waking hours pouring out her heart to God. After the negotiations proceeded it became obvious that the lack of a bribe would prevent the signing of the papers. Ben and Sherri had agreed to be adamant on that issue, believing a bribe would not give God the glory. As Sherri left the office and started up the hill, she began to weep uncontrollably. Her heavy heart made the walk back seem longer and more difficult than before.

Sherri's attorney grieved with her over the unproductive journey, but she promised to bring about a reversal. When Sherri finally heard from her after some delay, she learned that a return trip to the village would be necessary. This time, however, Sherri could not take little Abby along, because it was too hard on her. In addition, she learned that a plane was going into that area and seats were available. The best news, though, came in the form of a call from Ben. He was coming! Friends in Kathmandu volunteered to keep Abby, and they were on their way. The group consisted of Sherri, Ben, the attorney, her friend, and the birth father.

The second visit to the official's office the next morning proceeded without a hitch. Returning to Kathmandu with the needed signature, the attorney tended to the remaining paper work, and Sherri arranged for Abby's travel documents. They later learned that theirs was the only adoption the attorney was able to complete that summer. As they left the airport, Sherri remembered the prayer she had offered earlier: "Lord, next time we leave this airport, please let our child be with us." A gracious God.

On a bulletin board in Abby's room in Hong Kong you can see the photographs of the dozens of friends who prayed for Sherri and Ben through those two-and-a-half months. In the center you will see, "For this child I prayed, and the Lord has given me my petition which I asked of him, 1 Samuel 1:27 NKJV." Ask Sherri if Abby is worth the risk, and see her light up!

Risking Life, Limb and Reputation
Lorry Lutz, author of *Women as Risk-Takers for God*, shares thrilling stories of faithful women of the church. These women were willing to bear Christ's message even when it posed threats to their lives and standing. Women were vitally involved in the early church. Paul lists ten women in Romans 16, identifying some as "fellow-workers," a term which he used normally to describe male workers in the church. Lutz traces the history of women denying personal fortune and using their wealth instead for ministry and others who faced

death and persecution. After providing these examples of brave women in history, she inspires us with the stories of modern-day risk-takers all over the world.

Being a risk-taker does not guarantee adulation or even success. To the contrary, many heroic efforts for Christ's sake court disaster. In some countries of the world, to be known as a Christian results in expulsion or even death. Laws in those lands prohibit the gathering of Christians, the propagating of their beliefs, and even owning a Bible.

In spite of threats Christians in these parts of the world often meet secretly and mutually strengthen one another in the spirit of the Lord. They trust the Father to guide them through the treacherous waters of persecution and courageously risk all to be faithful.

Christian missionaries look danger in the face when they follow their call to troubled spots. Many countries are closed to the gospel, and to bear a Christian witness is punishable by death. In spite of the risk, courageous missionaries find ways to enter those countries in order to share the witness of Christ. Knowing the danger and the consequences of being found out, they nevertheless obey God's command to teach and baptize all who desire to follow our Lord, Jesus Christ.

"Blessed are those who are persecuted for righteousness' sake, for theirs is the kingdom of heaven. Blessed are you when people revile you and persecute you and utter all kinds of evil against you falsely on my account. Rejoice and be glad, for your reward is great in heaven, for in the same way they persecuted the prophets who were before you" (Matthew 5:10–11).

Young people, students in universities and colleges, give up a summer or a semester to volunteer in difficult places, hoping to plant a seed, to influence one person for our Christ. Others enter seamy areas of the inner city in our own country, risking their very lives, to bear Christ's witness to the down-and-out.

For a number of years Christian Women's Job Corps® units have been established across the US to assist women in becoming financially sufficient and finding the "abundant life" as well. Today some of these ministries target prostitutes and exotic dancers as well as soon-to-be-released inmates in prisons and jails. Not only do the teachers and mentors risk their personal safety, they place their reputation in peril as well. Some would perhaps say, "But what will people think?" Yet the incarnate Christ exemplified the risk of radical discipleship. Can we do less?

A Short Manual for Risk-Taking

As we consider these women who have risked much, we are struck by the elements they hold in common.

First, they were passionate. How do you know when a change or an idea is worth the fight? When it becomes a passion in your life. When it fills your thoughts day and night. Rosa Parks lived more than forty years drinking at designated fountains, being excluded from events and buildings. When faced one more time with going to the back of the bus, she had had it. She rejected a lifetime of prejudice because of the fire in her heart.

Second, they sought others who were like-minded. One high school student praying at the flagpole would have little effect, but when youth all over the US gather at multiple flagpoles to pray, it makes a statement. The suffragists discovered that as they involved diverse groups in their cause, they strengthened their position. Sherri sought people who would pray for her and Ben, knowing that the secret of all risk-taking is the power of God. No one should embark on an uncertain and fearful journey without first recruiting faithful and intentional prayer warriors on her behalf.

Third, our risk-takers were clear about their purpose. Rosa Parks knew that her refusal to yield her seat on the bus would not go unnoticed. The founders of MADD had one solitary goal: to prevent the destruction that alcohol causes. The narrower the focus, the easier it is to communicate. A vision statement and goals keep the purpose ever before the participants.

Fourth, our risk-takers developed a plan. Deborah enacted God's plan, the best pattern of all. "For surely I know the plans I have for you, says the Lord, plans for your welfare and not for harm, to give you a future with hope" (Jeremiah 29:11). He has promised to reveal His plan to those who ask. When we go off willy-nilly without having surveyed the field, assessing our assets, and developing a strategy, we have little hope for success.

Fifth, they counted the cost. Jesus warned His followers to consider the cost of discipleship before starting a pilgrimage. The price tag is not always reflected by the dollar mark. Time, physical health, zeal, and thick skin may be more valuable to a cause than money. Deborah's risk was to the death. Missionaries, too, know the chances they take in following God's call to a difficult place. They rely upon our prayers for safety and wisdom.

Sixth, the risk-takers motivated others. Rosa Parks' resistance and arrest set off a boycott on the bus system for more than a year. Blacks and whites banded together behind her to make a statement. They would walk to work, to church, and to shop rather than step one foot into a bus.

Seventh, they avoided rigidity. When World War I began, the suffragists put their work aside in order to support the country in its war efforts. The leaders of MADD have refashioned the focus of their program to meet specific needs related to the abuse of alcohol. They currently design programs of alcohol awareness directed to teens.

Finally, these risk-takers persevered. Many good efforts are begun but not sustained, and the dream dies. The roaring fire slowly fades into embers for lack of fuel. Discouragement, distractions, and lost vision rob us of the joy of the fulfillment of a goal. Each failure causes us to think twice about stepping out again. None of our risk-takers found instant success. The leaders of the suffragist movement worked for seventy-five years before earning the right to vote, and some of its faithful workers died never having cast the first ballot. Any quest worth following is fraught with risks and detours, but oh! the sweet rewards to those who endure.

Perhaps you have had a "fire in your belly" about some issue but have not had the courage or direction to follow through. Fan the flames! Seek wisdom from God. Examine your motives. Look at options and acceptable compromises. Make wise choices for your involvement and seek reliable sources for advice. Pray much. And give God the glory.

"Wait for the Lord;
be strong, and let your heart take courage;
wait for the Lord!"
(Psalm 27:14)

CHAPTER 5

Seeking Justice

When I was hungry, you offered me food,
When I was thirsty, you gave me drink,
When I was a stranger, you opened your door,
When I was naked, your coat I wore.

I was imprisoned, you came to my cell,
Stood by my bedside when I lay ill,
Though I disguised it, you still knew my face,
Now come, oh blessed, claim your right place.
—Source unknown

"Mommy, are we rich?" our daughter Erin shouted as she slammed the back screen door. She had been visiting her little friend in the *kampung* near our house. *Kampungs* are neighborhoods of small houses found in every city and village in Indonesia. Many of the *kampung* houses then were simple bamboo structures with dirt floors, and had neither electricity nor indoor plumbing. Furnishings were spartan; a kerosene lantern provided light when necessary.

The dreaded question hung heavy in the air. Of course, to Erin's friend there was no question at all. We had a house with many rooms, not just one like the house she and her whole family lived in. We had screens on the windows to keep the malaria-carrying mosquitoes out, and ceiling fans to bring some relief from the tropical heat. Electricity provided light and power for numerous appliances. Dozens of garments filled our closets.

I had to laugh at the irony of it. Just days before, a

woman visiting from the US entered our kitchen with her nose wrinkled up in a disbelieving grimace. "What is that smell? Kerosene? Do you have to cook with kerosene?" Given the choices of wood, bottled gas, or kerosene, we opted for the last. Our guest was more surprised to observe that we not only cooked with kerosene but also boiled all the water we drank. She certainly would not have considered us "rich."

Yet by the world's standard, we were rich. In the early part of the 1960s the average annual income per capita in Indonesia was three hundred dollars. Thanks to the warm temperatures and ample rainfall, food was abundant and sustained even the poor. Poverty was a cruel presence, however, in Indonesia as well as other places around the world.

Many years later and many miles from Indonesia, Erin's question, "Are we rich?" surfaced again in my mind as I listened to a woman tell of her own past. She was the first child born to the town drunk and his wife in a little town in Louisiana. If she looked down in the shack where she lived, she could see the chickens through the cracks in the floor. Through the breaks in the roof she could see the stars. Never once could she remember her mother holding her on her lap and telling her she loved her.

She and her seven younger siblings endured much taunting and humiliation because of the mess her father had made of his life. Finally, he was so disabled by his addiction he could no longer support his family. Her mother took a job to provide for her children's needs, the daughter dropped out of school and became the surrogate mother. She washed the clothes, cooked, and cleaned the house in order to keep the family going. No time—no energy—for school. Just grow up!

One day an older woman in her church began coming to see her. She taught her to cook nutritious meals and to plant flowers to make the surroundings more beautiful. She told her about a God who loved her and wanted her to become a part of His family. "I couldn't believe it! The great God loved me! I hardly dared believe it." But she accepted this marvelous love offered by her new master, Jesus.

One day, when she was much older, she decided to take matters of the heart into her own hands. Sadie Hawkins Day was coming, she got into her pickup, drove to the house of a young man she liked, and asked him for a date. To her surprise and great joy he accepted; later he asked her for a date. During the next months, they became aware of their deep mutual love, and agreed that God could use them together in marriage. "But," he said, "you will have to be a pastor's wife, because God has called me to the ministry." She tried to imagine the kind of life he pictured, but the leap seemed too great.

Telling the rest of the story many years later, she appeared before us a winsome, confident, and competent pastor's wife. Difficult as it was to reconcile the "before-and-after" images, she clearly had risen from the ashes of her early life. Not every poor woman, however, is so fortunate.

Rich Woman—Poor Woman?

The status of women varies enormously depending upon their location in the world. In the least-developed countries in Africa, the Middle East, Asia, and Latin America, overwhelming poverty coupled with long-standing patterns of discrimination create difficult living conditions for women.

How did God decide where to put each of us in His world? Did He deliberately choose to give some of us parents who loved us and could give us the "good life"? Did He select a country where we would have all the facilities to train us for life and work? It would follow then, would it not, that He just as intentionally fashioned a family fathered by a town drunk and doomed to live in poverty? Or perhaps one's fate is randomly determined, a kind of human roulette to see who can beat the odds. Have you ever wondered why you were not born in some poverty-stricken area of the world? How would your life differ had you been placed in a family of another religion—one that demeaned girls and women?

Almost all women love to try on clothes. For the next few minutes, let's try on roles of women around the world and try to imagine our lives if the transfer were real and permanent.

If I Were a Poor Girl

Nepal has never been an easy place for a woman, especially if she is poor. Some 1600 years ago a woman gave money to finance a trust to carry out religious observances. Her inscription on the Buddhist *stupa* near Kathmandu concludes with this wish: "Let me, as a result of this virtuous deed, be born as a man in my next birth."

As bad as things were for women in Nepal then, they are not much better now. Today many young girls in Nepal are tricked into leaving home, sometimes even sold by their poverty-stricken families. Duped into believing they will go to India to earn money working in the rug factories or as maids, they are instead sold into prostitution. Forced to work in filthy brothels, they provide cheap sexual services to lorry (truck) drivers and migrant workers. Condoms are never used to protect the women, so they often contract sexually transmitted diseases. No longer able to do their "job," they are thrown out of the brothel. Untrained for any other work, they cannot provide for themselves. Ashamed of their daughters, their families often refuse to receive them back home. Sick and with no remaining options, the bereft women literally have no place to go. The birth of a girl into a poor Nepali family brings little joy.

Deborah (not her real name) serves in a country where female trafficking is a huge problem. She is part of an educational effort there that works to put an end to this practice. In the meantime, she works alongside others to provide safe haven for those abused women.

Deborah first saw the results of "flesh trade" when she joined another American and nine nationals on a survey trip to the country where young girls are taken after being sold. Husbands, fathers, brothers, or uncles, for a small price (by Western standards), had sold most of them. Some were sold because they were one of many daughters, and the family could not afford the dowries. Others were dispensable because they had never borne sons or because the husband had taken another wife and she was no longer "needed." For some the sale provided money to buy a new roof on the house.

When Deborah visited the brothels, she was appalled. A three-year-old child lived under a bed, never allowed to go outside—an innocent victim of her mother's misfortune. Young women were held captive and abused until they became a liability for their "owners," having been infected by men with HIV/AIDS.

The visiting group was pleased to find that a national Christian in that country had begun a ministry to these poor women. In weekly group meetings many had experienced soul freedom in Christ, but physically they remained captive in a despicable situation. When Deborah's group returned home, they began to formulate a plan for getting the girls out of the country and home again. Fifteen months later, eight women were rescued and returned. Because their families would not receive them back, they were placed in a home provided by Deborah's group. Once housing was arranged, the young women began to learn cottage industry skills that would enable them to become self-sufficient.

This is not the end, of course. The most unfortunate are those HIV/AIDS positive women who now require hospice-type care. Their only consolation is the confidence that they now have an eternal home where abuse and hopelessness do not overcome. They now know new life and true healing in a mighty God and Savior.

Imagine living in the slums of any third-world country, going to sleep each night cold, hungry, and bone-tired. Will there be work tomorrow, and will the money earned be enough? What will happen to the children with no one to watch them throughout the day, and no medicine when they're sick? Yet each year the missed period brings despair. The following days of nausea and months of discomfort confirm the reality. Then it comes, one more mouth to feed from an empty breast and bare cupboard. No matter, it will probably die in time.

Some parents in desperation simply throw the children away like a dirty sponge, no longer useful, just taking up space. Others see each child, no matter how young, as bait to lure in pennies by the wealthier constituents. The United Nations estimates that 150 million street children are found worldwide. Ranging in age from three to eighteen, about forty percent are homeless, an unprecedented number in the world's history. The other sixty percent work on the streets to support their families. While on the streets, these defenseless children fall victim to brutal violence, sexual exploitation, chemical addiction, and human rights violations.

Charlotte Greenhaw knew that thousands of street children lived in her city of Recife, Brazil. God kept reminding her of the verses in Matthew 25:

"For I was hungry and you gave me something to eat, I was thirsty and you gave me something to drink, I was a stranger and you invited me in, I needed clothes and you clothed me, I was sick and you looked after me, I was in prison and you came to visit me" (vv. 35–36 NIV).

Believing that these words were her call to minister to the street children, she set out to see what needed to be done. She learned that some of the "glue-sniffing" street children clustered near a Catholic church in a nearby neighborhood. They carried glue bottles, because inhaling the strong smell took away their appetites. With no money to buy food they could survive for a few more days. She immediately began to envision a children's choir of street children singing a Christmas cantata and hearing about the Father's love, a message they had never heard.

Charlotte found the children, sat down on the sidewalk with her keyboard in her lap, and began to sing. Within seconds she was surrounded by twenty filthy children, holding little bottles of glue in their hands. That was the beginning of her street children's choir, which met twice a week on the sidewalk. Eventually, the priest became her friend and the women of the church began a ministry with the children, allowing them to take baths and giving them food. Some were placed in schools; others found jobs. Their lives began to change through the songs they learned about Jesus, and some invited Him into their hearts.

In other places of the world girls and women endure pagan practices so gruesome that they are seldom made known. In the Middle East and Africa between eight and ten million women and girls are at risk of undergoing female genital mutilation (FGM). Practiced also in the Muslim areas of Indonesia and Malaysia, it is part of a ceremonial induction into adult society. Sometimes referred to erroneously as "female circumcision," it is far more drastic and damaging than male circumcision. It includes the removal of functioning parts of the genitalia with unclean sharp instruments such as razor blades, scissors, kitchen knives, and pieces of glass. Antiseptic and anesthesia are seldom used. The unnecessary procedure is performed when the little girl is sometimes as young as three years old, but mutilated women suffer the medical consequences throughout their adult lives.

Why would parents insist that this horrendous operation be performed on their daughters? To perpetuate customs which seek to regulate and keep control over the body and sexuality of females. Would you believe that ten thousand girls are at risk of this practice in the US each year? Because of the serious results of FGM, Congress passed a bill outlawing it in the fall of 1994. Even though FGM is practiced mostly in Islamic countries, it is not an exclusively Islamic practice. Amazingly it is found across cultures, among Coptic Christians, Protestants, Catholics, and indigenous groups. Though efforts are being made to rid the entire world of this scandalous practice, countless women endure its agony every year.

Worldwide one billion people have no access to health care. The area of the world most at risk for lack of health care is sub-Saharan Africa. Because of the AIDS epidemic, the age expectancy of babies born today is forty years or less. Compare that to the age expectancy for women in the US, who live twice that long. According to a report from the *New York Times*, 2.4 million Africans died of AIDS in 2000, and it is expected to claim the lives of about half of all fifteen-year-olds. More than 25 million Africans are now living with HIV, the virus that causes AIDS.

Lack of health care goes hand in hand with poverty. The Population Institute says that 1.3 billion people live in absolute poverty, surviving on less than a dollar a day. Eighty-five countries are unable to grow or purchase enough food to provide for their populations. As a result, 840 million people are malnourished.

Education is one of the greatest forces for positive change in women's lives. The good news is that even in the poorest countries the impressive investment made by the governments in education are paying off. The availability of education and health care, including birth control, remain the two most important factors determining the quality of life for women. Without them our sisters around the world face a hopeless future.

A Brief Intermission
An intermission? And none too soon, you must be saying. We can only stand so much gloom and doom.

When I was a little girl, I looked forward each week to the movies on Saturday afternoon. I didn't always get to go, but I always *looked forward* to it. In those days commercial entertainment was hard to come by. During the week the children in my neighborhood played outside games like "kick the can," "Red Rover," and sports—baseball, football (yes, even I played), and tennis. No Little League organized us into teams, and no parent served as official. Disputed transgressions of the rules were resolved with much shouting and threatening to "go home." If it were raining or too cold, we opted for board games inside, playing duets on the piano, or listening to "Portia Faces Life," "Fibber McGee and Molly," or other radio shows.

But Saturday at the movies was the real treat! The little marquee on top of the theater and the posters in the front told us the name of the movie that was showing—just one. We could not have imagined a choice of six or ten or more. I can still remember being scared out of my wits by *The Hunchback of Notre Dame* and captivated by anything in which Elizabeth Taylor starred.

The beginning time of the feature was not important, because when we paid for our tickets we expected to be there for some time. In addition to the main feature, we saw a cartoon and a "short" segment on various topics, sometimes funny, sometimes informative. A "serial" followed (or preceded, depending on when you came in), usually a cowboy, or "oater" for you crossword addicts. Movies (a long and a short), cartoon and serial—not too skimpy an offering for nine cents! Also included in the price was a newsreel giving us a look at the events of our day. (No television, remember.) While adults probably enjoyed even that, for kids it was popcorn time.

News in the '40s and '50s was all about war, crime, and disease. Sounds like today, right? Since that time, however, most of the problems of that day have been resolved. Japan and Germany are now our allies. Smallpox has been eradicated and polio is a thing of the past. In the intervening years other enemies have risen up and been "picked off" like wooden ducks at a shooting arcade. Khrushchev, banging his shoe on the table at the UN, made us believe communism would bury us. Today the hammer and sickle guide Cuba and North Korea, hardly the world giants we feared in the past.

Every era has its own Goliaths, threatening for a time and then disappearing to be replaced by others. But never without resistance. An enemy not defied digs in and takes residence. The first step in its displacement is recognition of its presence.

Thus we continue to examine our world, the larger part with all its thorns, for we are part and parcel of its problems and their solutions. Further, as Christian women we are able to offer eternal hope for all humankind. Can we just sit back and stay uninvolved?

Windows in the Sky

In 2 Kings 7 we find the compelling story of four lepers living outside Samaria's city gate. Besieged by Ben-Hadad's entire army from Aram, the people within Samaria's walls were starving. So great was the famine that the people resorted to eating unclean animals and even to cannibalism.

In a heated encounter with Elisha, a messenger from the king of Samaria shouted, "This trouble is from the Lord! Why should I hope in the Lord?"

The man of God replied with an incredible prophecy, "Tomorrow about this time a measure of choice meal shall be sold for a shekel, and two measures of barley for a shekel at the gate." No one could imagine such unbelievably reduced prices, according to that day's inflated exchange.

"Even if the Lord were to make windows in the sky, could such a thing happen?" remarked the captain sent by the king.

"You shall see it with your own eyes, but you shall not eat from it."

Meanwhile, the lepers considered their grim prospects. "What shall we do? If we enter the city, what would we find there? With no food, we would only die. But if we stay here, we shall also die. Let's go to the Arameans. If they spare our lives, we live. If they kill us—well, we'll die anyway. We have no other choice."

So early in the morning they entered the Aramean camp. No one in the camp stirred. As they crept closer, they detected no movement.

"What is this? You'd think someone would be guarding the camp. And surely the cooks would be preparing the morning meal. Look! The horses and donkeys are leashed. Maybe it's a trap. They saw us approaching and plan an ambush."

They ventured closer. One brave leper sneaked up to the nearest tent and cautiously pulled back the flap. Without uttering a word, he went to the next tent, and the next. Motioning to the others to follow, they entered every tent to discover no one was there. Apparently, the Arameans had fled with haste, leaving their clothes and food behind. And silver and gold! Plunder taken from other campaigns had also been abandoned.

What the men did not know was that the Lord had caused the Aramean soldiers to hear the sound of chariots and horses in the night. Fearing that a huge army of paid Hittite and Egyptian mercenaries had come to destroy them, they fled, taking nothing.

With whoops of joy and shouts of glee, the lepers ate and drank to their hearts' content. They tried on several robes to find which ones fit. Nubs that once were hands caressed the fine fabric. After wearing rags for so long, even the uniforms of the soldiers felt grand. As for the silver, gold, and other valuables, they would just have to bury them to be retrieved at a later time.

Suddenly, one man stopped. "Wait. What are we doing? This is not right. This is a day of good news; if we are silent and wait until the morning light, we will be found guilty; therefore let us go and tell the king's household."

The king listened in disbelief. Suspicious of an ambush, he sent a complement of his troops on the horses, those that had not been eaten, to investigate. This group found even more garments and valuables thrown away by the fast-retreating Aramean soldiers.

Within minutes word spread inside the city gates. Alerted to food and treasure free for the taking, the people swarmed over the abandoned camp. The reinforcement of food and drink and the acquisition of new wealth brought economic stability to the community. The prices on barley, meal, and all commodities plummeted, just as Elisha had said. The Lord had indeed opened windows in the sky.

And the captain who questioned Elisha's prediction? He was trampled to death by the people at the gate.

Out of Sight, Out of Mind

Like the lepers, we have been surrounded by a blessed life we did not earn. Born in a land that honors freedom and goodwill, we have been protected from persecution and criminal acts. Our American lifestyle is the envy of the world. The strong economy enables most citizens to eat well and enjoy adequate housing. Education is free and even mandated to every child. Available and inexpensive electricity allows illumination and comfortable temperatures in our ample houses, regardless of the weather outside. Adequate fuel supplies keep America's cars on the excellent roads and highways. Religious freedom is guaranteed by the Constitution, even permitting the evangelizing and seeking of converts.

Among the wealthiest nations in the world, we enjoy a quality of life inaccessible to most people. Like the lepers in the presence of wealth free for the taking, we work in a frenzy to accumulate more and more. Our tables are laden with the most delicious food, our bodies adorned with the latest styles and jewelry. What we cannot spend immediately we bank and invest. We revel in our good fortune.

Isn't some Christian woman cued to say, "Wait! What are we doing? This is not right. This is a day of good news." We live on an island of great wealth, surrounded by a sea of want. Can we be content to continue hoarding things for ourselves while others are going down for the third time—many of them our brothers and sisters in Christ?

Thankfully, efforts are being made to relieve these injustices against upon women and children around the world. Our government is assisting the UN by providing funds to combat the trafficking of women and children in South Asia. These monies assist grassroots, national, and regional Non-Governmental organizations to strengthen law enforcement and provide shelters and rehabilitative programs for female victims of trafficking. Missions agencies have also joined efforts in rehabilitating victims of trafficking. International agencies have focused on the problem of street children, but the difficulty persists. Missionaries like Charlotte Greenhaw, seeing the atrocities up close, have determined to do what they can in their own areas.

International poverty is fought on many levels. Bread for the World is a nonpartisan organization supported by 45 denominations. Its 45,000 members lobby Congress and the administration to bring about public policy changes that address the root causes of hunger and poverty in the US and overseas. BFW's present goal is to call upon our government and its allies to commit to a global plan to cut world hunger in half by 2015. This plan is called "Hunger to Harvest." Bread for the World's research discovered that by increasing poverty assisstance by $4 billion by benefactor nations, that goal could be reached. Imagine reducing the world's hunger by half—all at a cost of one penny per every American per day!

Your church may participate in a world hunger offering. This money enables agricultural missionaries to assist farmers in many countries to apply more productive techniques to increase their yields. The digging of water wells and purification of unsafe water provide easier and healthier lives for many.

Human need moved the heart of our Lord. He let it be known early that compassion drove His ministry:

"The Spirit of the Lord is upon me,
because he has anointed me
to bring good news to the poor.
He has sent me to proclaim release to the captives
and recovery of sight to the blind,
to let the oppressed go free,
to proclaim the year of the Lord's favor."
(Luke 4:18–19)

Doing justice is not a project, and loving mercy is not without cost. To know God, truly know Him, is to claim His same love and tender compassion for all people. While His ultimate concern is for the salvation of each person's soul, He would not neglect the tragedies faced in this world. Nor can we.

Do Justice, Love Mercy

When we were living in Indonesia, mail was extremely important. Bill went to the post office every day when the mail was distributed in his eagerness to receive word from our friends and loved ones back home. He was picturing a box full and overflowing with the treasured letters, when something caught his eye. A child lay motionless on the porch. Someone had dropped coins, another some pieces of bread. The boy had been unable to take advantage of either.

Bill began to ask the people passing by, but no one seemed to know who the boy was or how he had come to be there. Since no offer of assistance seemed available, Bill lifted the thin, emaciated, and unconscious body of the child into our car. When he carried him into the hospital, the admission staff seemed reluctant to receive him. Bill continued to impress upon them the obvious need of the child for medical help, but still they hesitated. "You know, sir, that you could have found hundreds of others just like him."

"Yes," said Bill, "but I found *this* one, and he needs our help. Obviously, we cannot save hundreds, but how can we avoid giving assistance even to this one?" With those words of persuasion the admission personnel accepted him.

Observation and testing confirmed that Samin, the name chosen for him by hospital personnel, was retarded as a result of chronic malnutrition and lack of care. After he was released from the hospital, Samin entered a facility for children with special needs, which had been carefully selected by Bill.

Micah offered this summary statement regarding God's expectations of us: "He has told you, O mortal, what is good; and what does the Lord require of you but to do justice, and to love kindness, and to walk humbly with your God?" (Micah 6:8).

Several years ago I was a part of a group of women involved in two immersion experiences. One took us to Chicago to survey Christian ministries in that diverse urban culture. The second was a study of poverty in the Appalachian area of the US. The two experiences demonstrated the diversity of life in America, but we also noted similarities. One commonality buried itself in our hearts like a sticker in a West Texas pasture. In both urban and rural settings, women were trapped in poverty with no way to extricate themselves. The Holy Spirit made it clear that a ministry to those women was needed, and Christian Women's Job Corps®, a welfare-to-work ministry for women, was born.

If we had stayed in our offices and homes, we might have missed the joy of having a part in seeing women redeemed from both a human and a spiritual stand-point.

Earlier in this chapter you were asked to try on different roles of women around the world. We discovered again how constricting they were. Blessed beyond measure, we want to do justice and love mercy in our day. In Paul's brief letter to the Colossians he gives advice for believers who seek fullness of life in Christ.

"As God's chosen ones, holy and beloved, clothe yourselves with *compassion, kindness, humility, meekness,* and *patience*. Above all, clothe yourselves with *love*, which binds everything together in perfect harmony" (Colossians 3:12,14, emphasis mine).

God requires that we dress ourselves in garments of justice and mercy, designed long ago but still fashionable in our day.

CHAPTER 6
Upholding Racial Reconciliation

God, make me color blind,
so I can see mankind as Jesus does.
Bring to each empty hour
the motivating pow'r of Jesus' call.
When man has done me wrong
help me to suffer long as Jesus did.
And when the road is rough,
Lord, make my strength enough to follow Him.
Give me the grace to go through hell
so man may know that Jesus loves.
—Bill O'Brien, From the song "The Namegivers"

My husband penned these words in the late 1960s. Physical color blindness, the inability to distinguish among some colors, is an inconvenience for some. In the spiritual realm, however, color blindness can be a wonderful thing, a goal to be reached. God told Samuel that while humans tend to give value to the outer appearance, He looks at the inner person (1 Samuel 16:7). Few of us can avoid forming opinions based on our initial impression of another person—how she is dressed, arranges her hair, walks.

At a national conference for school administrators, the leader instructed us to move from one group to reconfigure a new group. He told us also not to say anything, but to take our seats. Too late. I had already said "hi" to several people. Our assignment was to watch as each member walked silently around the group and then write a paragraph based on our assumptions— where they lived, where they went to school, what position they held in school. I had said only one word, but they had me nailed—I was recognized as a southerner and the rest was easy.

Regional stereotypes abound in our country and around the world. Northeasterners live in the fast lane, southwesterners are all cowboys, southerners are rather slow. Americans are rich, Asians are smart, Africans live in the jungle and fight wild animals. Lacking personal acquaintance with people from these areas, we allow others to form our opinions based on erroneous information. Stereotyping and categorizing individuals based on place of origin, color, or creed robs us of meaningful relationships with some of the world's finest people. What's more, prejudice does not find a comfortable fit in the heart of a believer.

Today we are blessed to live among a racially diverse population in America. People of many races and cultures now populate even small towns that not so many years ago were home only to one racial group. Schools and workplaces are integrated. Shopping malls and places of entertainment welcome us all to enter their doors. We live in a multicultural haven—or so it would seem. But in the midst of the apparent goodwill among races, injustice still exists. As Christian women we must be aware of racism and how we can work to eradicate it.

We Have to Learn
The kindergarten class resembled an ant colony, swarming over numerous pieces of school playground equipment. Engaged as the children were during the morning recess, they hardly noticed when a car ducked into a

visitor's parking place. When their eyes focused on the lady getting out of the car, however, they began to rush toward her, excitedly asking questions.

"Hi. Whose mother are you? Is the birthday cake for us? Who has a birthday today?" Innocent questions, until we know that in the kindergarten class the students are all Anglo—except one little African American boy who was obviously the birthday boy. How do we know? You guessed it. His mother was also African American. It never occurred to them that by the process of elimination, they could figure the answers out all by themselves.

Children are slow to make inferences by the color of one's skin. In *South Pacific*, a Rodgers and Hammerstein musical, the song "You've Got to Be Taught" speaks of early lessons in discrimination based on color:

> *You've got to be taught before it's too late,*
> *Before you are six or seven or eight,*
> *To hate all the people your relatives hate—*
> *You've got to be carefully taught.*

Often children simply adopt their parents' attitudes toward people of color as they learn other patterns of response, but sometimes the more effective teachers are their own peers.

In 1962, Leon and Anne Mitchell were in Dallas on furlough from their mission post in Indonesia. Everything was new to their children, since the last four years had been in a radically different environment. Leon and Anne smiled at their expressions of joy in newfound experiences in playmates, toys, foods, and school. Every day brought fresh insights. It was good to be home again, even for a year. As Christmas approached, Anne took five-year-old Leland along with her to run several errands.

"Know what I'm going to ask Santa Claus to bring me for Christmas?" Before Anne could speak, he answered his own question. "A gun."

Anne could hardly believe her ears. "Why do you need a gun?" she managed to reply. Leland told her that he was going to shoot a black person who lived on the creek. But he used a racial epithet to refer to the man, possibly not even realizing that he referred to a person.

Anne was horrified. At that time they were driving through a predominantly black neighborhood. She asked him if he had ever seen one of those type people.

Leland, sensing the tension in the air, merely shook his head "no," waiting in wide-eyed expectation for what was to come.

"How do you know one lives on the creek?" Anne did her best to keep her voice calm.

"My friend told me."

Then Anne lost it. She told her son that was not a nice word to refer to black people, and he was not to use it again. She realized that his peers had planted the seeds of hate and that from now on her teaching must be more overt, more direct, to counter what he was learning from them. Later she discovered through her next-door neighbor, a wonderful Christian woman, that an elderly black man sometimes camped on the creek when the weather was nice.

Anne is quick to tell you that Leland did not get a gun that Christmas. Today he is a policeman and protects all residents of Abilene, Texas—regardless of race.

How did you formulate a personal position on the issue of race? That answer may depend on where and when you spent your formative years. Living in a west

Texas city where few African Americans resided, my opinions were few and based on what I heard from others. The larger number of Hispanics in my school, still a small percentage of the student body, kept to themselves. Only when I entered college did I ever have personal contact with African Americans, but the exposure was minimal.

In January 1958, my husband accepted a position on a church staff in Carlsbad, New Mexico. Since it was the middle of the school year, no teaching positions were open for me. However, the school administration expressed a need to give additional support to the newly integrated school in the district. Would I teach music in the morning and a third-grade class in the afternoon? I really needed the job, and I agreed. The school, I learned, had formerly been the school for black elementary students. The "integration" involved bringing Hispanic children to form the mix. One little blond girl was the sole Anglo. The principal was black; the teachers were equally divided between white and black. A few teachers had requested to go there; some were sent there by the school administration. I taught there for a year, until a full-time position became available.

Would I have deliberately chosen such an experience? God only knows, but the fact He did not allow me a choice makes me wonder. He knew I needed that learning opportunity. When the year was over, I knew it too. Never again would a child of color escape my notice. "Red and yellow, black and white, they are precious in His sight," and mine, too.

Baby boomers or busters could hardly relate to my experience. They've probably attended school with African Americans, Hispanics, and Asians. Through more effective school integration and the burgeoning numbers of immigrants, America's school population has become increasingly diverse.

For the nonwhite population of the mid-century in the South, however, life was much different from my insulated experience.

That Was Then

Life was tough for African Americans growing up in the US in the early and mid-twentieth century. Though parents attempted to shield their children from the rebuffs, cruelty, and injustices, they found it impossible to protect them from ugly discrimination. Water fountains and toilets marked *For Whites Only* and entrance to restaurants, theaters, and public schools barred to them were daily reminders that they were different and unworthy somehow.

When Carrie Allen McCray, granddaughter of an ex-slave and a Confederate general, was seventy-three years old, she still remembered how bewildering it was. Why did they mistreat her so? Was there something wrong with her? Her poem "Red Balloons" reveals the deep wounds of segregation:

Red Balloons

Flapping signs read Gay's Dixie Carnival
Papa, could I have one of those red balloons.
My sister, innocent at five, did not know what she
was asking—but Papa did
that wonderful world of merry-go-round,
red balloons dancing in the hot southern breeze,
songs of summer in his eyes, he risked it any way,
stopped the car, went over to the carnival gate
Could he just have a red balloon for his little girl

The words of the carnival man as hard as his face
"Nigger ain' nuthin here for you or yourn"
Shaking her blond curls a little five-year-old
stuck her tongue out at Papa
Papa stood for a moment then back to the car
with promises of lots of red balloons when we get home
I was eight years old then but even now, whenever I
hear the sound of a carousel, I see Papa's wintered face
as he watched all the other fathers
taking their children through the gate.

—From the book *The Crimson Edge: Older Women Write, Vol. 1*, edited by Sondra
Zeidenstein (Chicory Blue Press, Goshen, Connecticut: 1996, pp 136-137. Used by
permission.)

The racial conflict, especially in the South, escalated in
the 1960s. Black sit-ins, marches, and other acts of
peaceful protest often evoked backlashes of ever more
serious racial crimes. Pictures of police with fire hoses
and vicious dogs attacking black youths and children
were in newspapers all over the world. Although there
were deadlier crimes, few were conceived and carried
out with such a purity of malice as the Sunday morning
bombing of the Sixteenth Street Baptist Church in
Birmingham, which killed four young girls.

News of the Birmingham church bombing traveled
quickly to Indonesia where Bill and I were living at the
time. In fact, word went out to every area of the globe,
damaging the evangelistic work of missionaries. For
many the inferred message that people of dark skin were
considered lower than the white race negated the
gospel message of God's love for all people. Sadly, in
many countries colonizers had already effectively prop-
agated the myth of racial superiority.

In Birmingham, what was meant to intimidate the blacks served instead to galvanize them and many others appalled by the tragic deaths of the little girls. The year 1965 brought passage of the Civil Rights Act, which set our nation on its still-unfinished course toward racial reconciliation.

This Is Now
Why bring up the past? Haven't we all paid a dear price for our earlier sins? Are there not now laws in place to give all races equal opportunity? Why make it a problem? We see encouraging signs indicating that racial tensions are being eased somewhat. True, since the '60s much progress has been made, but few would say that prejudice has been abolished.

African Americans have experienced three waves of "otherness" in this land of the free, each redefining their oppression. First Africans were brought to this country in chains as slaves. When slavery was abolished and slaves were freed, African Americans continued to live segregated lives. "Life, liberty and the pursuit of happiness" still eluded them, for a racist culture taught succeeding generations that African Americans are less than human. And now? The greatest obstacle to our African American brothers and sisters is lack of access. Blacks and whites continue to be separated by gaps of income, class and power, and while many in the power structure profess goodwill towards blacks, they resist allowing them access to this structure. The same is often true for America's increasing number of Hispanics as well.

Schoolbooks, supplies, and equipment in inner-city schools are frequently insufficient. Lack of computers and training in their use perpetuates lack of access for black youths. Poverty stands between many capable young black men and women and college degrees. Frustrated by limitations in their lives, they are easy prey to drugs, alcohol, and lives of crime. One of every three black men aged twenty to twenty-nine is incarcerated or on parole or probation. African Americans have the lowest ratio of marriage and the highest rate of divorce of all ethnic groups in the nation. Teenaged girls give birth to babies and fathers never acknowledge them.

One other fact implicates all of us. According to one study, racism is still alive and well. Researchers discovered that while the number is down from earlier years, twenty-five percent of the white population are "hardcore racists." What is more, a 1997 Gallup Poll reported that the church remains the one highly segregated major institution in America. Sociologist Orlando Patterson concluded, "The Christian church has failed miserably in the promotion of ethnic fellowship and is now the mainstay of segregation." How sad that Sunday is the most segregated day of the week! Do you not feel it strange that people of different races work together in secular endeavors, but cannot worship together on the Lord's Day?

America's black population has made huge advances. At the end of the twentieth century many of the most admired Americans were African Americans—Colin Powell, Michael Jordan, Oprah Winfrey. Tiger Woods won championships in all four of the most prestigious 2001 golf tournaments in America—a grand slam at age twenty-five. Spencer Perkins and Chris Rice, authors of *More Than Equals: Racial Healing for the Sake of the Gospel*, offer evidence that African Americans today are living more affluent and influential lives than at any time in our national experience.

Birmingham, Alabama, site of many of the shameful civil rights violations, home of "Bull" Connor, attacking dogs and fire hoses, is making a valiant effort to overcome its past. The Civil Rights Institute, dedicated to preserving the history of the movement, claims visitors from around the world. Many shed tears of shame and ask forgiveness. Young people, however, both Anglo and African American, often move through the displays almost aloof, unbelieving of the reality of that day.

In striving for a more just peace, more than 70,000 people have signed "The Birmingham Pledge," which states:

I believe that every person has worth as an individual. I believe that every person is entitled to dignity and respect, regardless of race or color. I believe that every thought and every act of racial prejudice is harmful; if it is my thought or act, then it is harmful to me as well as to others.

Therefore, from this day forward I will strive daily to eliminate racial prejudice from my thoughts and actions. I will discourage racial prejudice by others at every opportunity. I will treat all people with dignity and respect, and I will strive daily to honor this pledge, knowing that the world will be a better place because of my effort.

Many would say, "Let bygones be bygones; let's move on from the tragic mistakes of the past to a kinder future."

We do see signs of hope concerning reconciliation. But Perkins and Rice inject caution that whites and blacks reach completely "different conclusions from the same events and evidence. One mostly contends 'we've come so far,' the other, 'not yet.'" As Christian women we are called to commit to an ongoing struggle for full rights of people of all races.

Women as Reconcilers

We women must be able to follow Christ so intently that we become models in reconciliation. Before launching on such a noble cause, we must first assess our motives and our strengths and foibles. Perkins and Rice raise important questions for the Church today:

• If Jesus had the pulpit in your church next Sunday, what would he say is your Samaria—the people in the remotest part of your city or county, those you might have to work hardest to meet?
• What work is required to overcome the mistrust, fear and bitterness that are the residue of years of racial separation?
• How do we bring Christ and culture together into a church called to be one in mind and purpose?

To these questions we might add our own.

• If you were invited to a gathering in which you were to bring a friend of another ethnic group, do you have such a friend? Why or why not?
• Do you have opportunity to interact socially with women of other races? At work? At church?
• Would a person of another race feel comfortable attending your church? Your Sunday School? Why or why not?

Most of us have chosen churches where we can worship with those who speak our language, sing our songs, and have similar cultural backgrounds. Having made this choice, is it possible for us to become reconcilers? How can we show the world that Christians, regardless of race, are members of one family?

Lawton Higgs, a contemporary of mine, grew up in Arkansas. Everything he knew about people of color he learned at home, at school and at the church. First and foremost, he knew that black people diminished everything they touched. Property value declined when a black family moved in. Certainly, if they were allowed to enter either white schools or churches, they would bring about devaluation there as well.

When Lawton completed his degree at the university in 1966, he moved with Nancy, his wife, to Birmingham where he went to work at Alabama Power. They joined a large Methodist church in the city. On the heels of the worst of the civil rights battles, the problems were still far from being solved. Policemen who served under Bull Connor and segregationist leaders of the city held influential roles in the church. The view of people of color that Lawton developed in Arkansas would not be challenged here. He did, however, discover a truth that tested his theology. He had always thought that if your beliefs were correct and you did the right things, your salvation was guaranteed. Someone introduced him to the writings of John Wesley and he learned of the grace that brings salvation. "Since all have sinned and fall short of the glory of God; they are now justified by His grace as a gift, through the redemption that is in Christ Jesus" (Romans 3:23–24). He confessed for the first time that he could do nothing to secure his own salvation. God could and would provide him with full pardon and bring him into His family.

For some time Lawton had felt a call to preach, and three years after they had moved to Birmingham, he resigned his position and went to Candler Divinity School in Atlanta. It was there that he was again introduced to a writing that forever changed his life—Martin Luther King's "Letter from a Birmingham Jail." As he read it over and over he wept and cried out to God for forgiveness. Dr. King's statement of disappointment in the church that refused to stand up for godly principles convicted him of his own sinful stance.

Upon his graduation, Lawton and Nancy moved to Birmingham to pastor a church. In keeping with his commitment to church growth he hoped to build a great church there. One strategy he advocated: look for a moving van to find new residents and potential church members. One day, shortly after beginning his work, he noticed men unloading furniture and headed in their direction. But he stopped short when he caught a glimpse of the new residents; they were black. Lawton stood transfixed in the middle of the street. He heard God say, "Invite him to the church, Lawton." His feet felt like lead. Again God spoke, "Invite him to the church, Lawton."

When Lawton still hesitated, he felt as though God said, "Invite him to the church or go home and pack up. I can't use you here." The family did not come, of course. "They knew my invitation was not genuine," Lawton says. He had come so far, but the racial prejudice he had known his entire life was harder to overcome than he had thought. Through the next years black families did come, and many joined the church. "But it was really not an interracial church. We kept it a white church by the music we sang and the type of worship we planned." He longed for the time when he could pastor a church where people of any race or color could truly worship from their hearts.

Today Lawton pastors an interracial church in downtown Birmingham. He begins his personal testimony with "My name is Lawton Higgs. I'm a recovering racist."

A racist? Lawton has never been a member of the Klan nor knowingly contributed in any way to a criminal act toward a person of another race. But he, like many of us, confesses to past feelings of superiority and acts of discrimination.

Racial Reconciliation in Jesus' Day

Who could have predicted the events associated with Pentecost following Jesus' ascension? The prophet Joel did, and Peter quotes that passage in Acts 2:17–21. Even this prophecy of the coming of the Holy Spirit did not prepare His closest followers for the dramatic moment—a sound like a rushing wind, tongues of fire, and the ability to speak in other languages.

With the inspiration born of a new vision, Peter preached the truth to those gathered there. What an eclectic bunch! Medes, Persians, residents from Mesopotamia, Judea and Cappadocia, Egypt and Rome—people from near and far had come to Jerusalem for the Jewish Feast of Pentecost. Attracted by a sermon in their own language, they were soon captivated by this message of love and redemption. Three thousand new believers were added to the young church that day (Acts 2:41).

The miraculous, simultaneous translation of Peter's Passover message that day never occurred again as far as we know. It provided for a dramatic launch of the church. We assume many of the new Christians were only in Jerusalem for a few days. When they returned to their homes they carried the new seed of the church to their own peoples.

In Jerusalem the Holy Spirit continued to empower the church, and new members were added every day. Their communal living grew out of a strong sense of unity. Only one of the difficulties finds its way into the Scripture. Acts 6 relates the grievance of the Greek membership. Their widows were not receiving as large a part of the daily distribution of food as the Hebrew widows were. The work of the apostles in discipling the new Christians already demanded all their time. How could they also take on this new responsibility? They suggested instead that the Greek Jews select seven men of good standing, full of the Spirit and wisdom, whom they could appoint to this task. All was accomplished as the apostles wisely recommended, and the threat of racial conflict was avoided. The apostles very sensitively handled a delicate situation that could have become a divisive factor in the new church.

In the centuries following, church leaders dealt with other interracial issues, not always as successfully as the one in Jerusalem.

Today many churches still resist integration in their fellowships. Left to ourselves, we gravitate to those with similar interests, social standing, and worship style. What if the Holy Spirit led your church or mine to aggressively seek a connection, through membership or a partnership with another ethnic church? Would we have the courage to accomplish it?

Make It Happen
Once we have committed to be reconcilers according to God's command, we begin to change our patterns of

life. We become more aware of the persons of different ethnicity around us—at school, work, and in our daily lives. As we find out more about them, we enlarge our capacity to care and our desire to relate at deeper levels.

In relating to a wider circle of associates, God may lead you to be a catalyst in a closer understanding and appreciation of the group. Exchanged attendance in worship services, joint retreats, and social events give opportunity to interact on a deeper, more personal level with people of other ethnic groups. If a different language is spoken, learning words and phrases can be helpful. Cooking and eating ethnic foods together strengthens the relationship. Most of all, we pray that God will seal the friendship with His blessing.

God may send you His own special assignment as He did us. Eddie and Charlsetta Gibson fled their native land of Liberia when civil unrest escalated to civil war. For the second time in their married life, they left all their belongings behind and ran for their lives with their two small children. When they arrived in the US, they lived with us for several weeks. In circumstances such as this, families meld into one. My husband and I have been invited to attend and lead conferences for the large church where Eddie now serves as missions pastor. Their children's pictures adorn our refrigerator door, alongside our grandchildren. We are greatly enriched by the close ties with the Gibsons.

It's easy to continue in our usual patterns—same friends, same schedules. But we miss the tremendous blessings God has for us unless we step out to wider, more colorful vistas. Some churches have formed partnerships with other churches made up primarily of a different ethnic group. The partnerships are often created around a needed ministry. Members from two different congregations regularly tutor children in a nearby school, for example. A group of white and black churches in Mississippi formed an entity to assist church leaders in an African nation. One black congregation joined with a white one to send medical teams to South America.

One of my friends has been invited through the years to sites around the world to assist in setting up structures for non-formal education. He goes with one stipulation: the opportunity for him to learn from them will be built into the program as well. Too many times people are made to feel they are "mission objects." Full partnerships create trust in the endeavor.

Women do this so well. In countless places in the world I have experienced American women discussing a child, a piece of embroidery, or an ancient temple with another woman—with neither speaking the other's language! But the attempt to communicate across the language barrier with smiles, unorthodox sign language, and genuine "woman's intuition" speaks volumes. When the American guest gives her a cup of water or Scripture portion in her language, chances are it will be met with less suspicion and greater interest.

Fighting Complacency

It seems to me that the foe wielding the greatest power against reconciliation, however, is complacency. This voice convinces us that separation allows us each to be true to her own heritage. We feel comfortable with like-minded folks.

If we women look for "comfort," we have joined the wrong army. God has called us to forsake all to follow Him in a life that is the antithesis of ease and comfort. Our manual, the Bible, clearly states that all who share

God's grace are automatically commissioned to be agents of reconciliation.

Consider Ephesians 2:14–16: "For he is our peace; in his flesh he has made both groups [Jew and Gentile] into one and has broken down the dividing wall, that is, the hostility between us. He has abolished the law…that he might create in himself one new humanity in the place of the two, thus making peace, and might reconcile both groups to God in one body through the cross, thus putting to death that hostility through it."

"Aliens" and "strangers," our dog tags read. "Without hope and without God." But these terms are cancelled out, negated by the sacrifice of Christ. By His blood we are drawn together, disparate parts into union in Christ. He has broken down the barriers between us, completely overcoming the hostility between us. He has reconciled all of us into one body, a miracle bought by His precious blood. Now our statement of common identity reads "members of the household of God." The spiritual DNA that flows in the veins of our new family binds us all together.

When the twelve spies were sent out to survey Canaan, Numbers 13 and 14 tells us they returned with a unified report. They found a land flowing with milk and honey, and they carried clusters of grapes to prove it. The spies also agreed that fearsome giants inhabited the land and lived in highly fortified cities. The report threw the Israelites into a frenzy of fear. Panic really set in when Caleb urged the occupation of the land. In their homes they cried all night in hysteria. "Let's choose another leader and go back to Egypt," they decided in desperation.

The next day Caleb and Joshua repeated the report,

emphasizing the greatness of the Promised Land. Caleb added that if God were pleased with them, He would give them the land. "The Lord is with us; do not fear them," he concluded. We all know the people's response. Their fear called for the stoning of Caleb and Joshua. But when God appeared, a greater fear fell upon them. Only His mercy saved the people. "The Lord is slow to anger . . . forgiving iniquity and transgression" (Numbers 14:18). There would be, however, a price to pay for their lack of faith. Those who had gone out of Egypt and tested God in the wilderness would not be allowed to live to see the conquest.

God has trusted His message of reconciliation with His family. He asks that we remain one in Him, divisible by nothing, united in His love. The issue of racial reconciliation creates an overwhelming challenge for Christian women today. You can do your part by responding to these challenges:

• *Be informed about the issues.* Be alert to newspaper articles concerning racial discrimination in your area. Consider writing letters to the editor of your paper registering the need for racial reconciliation. Create a working group responsible for continued learning and work on Christian response on the issues of justice and reconciliation.

• *Remember that racial and intercultural harmony begins at home.* Discuss with your family the importance of relating to people of all cultures with kindness and respect. Intentionally develop strong friendships with persons of other races, and invite them into your home.

• *Pray for God's leadership in seeking to be used as an instrument of reconciliation.* Foster joint meetings with the women of your church and the women in church with members primarily of another race. Praying together about a common need or working together on a project creates a spirit of unity. Explore existing civil rights groups in your city as potential channels for your involvement.

• *Celebrate the diversity and uniqueness of others.* While adopting a common purpose and goal brings unity, pursuing diversity in personal interactions enriches our lives and brings joy to our hearts—and God's!

One day people of every tribe, language, and nation will bow down as one to worship our great God. But what about today? He can use us to be His instruments in our time. The task may not easy, but as in Caleb's time, even so in ours, God is with us. He will give us the victory. Reconciliation of all people, tribes, languages, nations is possible in Him. This is the time to claim the land for Him. Lead on, women. This is our hour.

CHAPTER 7

Nurturing Others

"I'm going to run to the card shop to pick up a birthday card for Kristen. Be back in a minute."

"Yeah, sure," my husband mumbles with a grin. He knows what all married men know. A woman can no more hurry the process of buying a greeting card than she can shorten the time for a cake to rise. Some things just take time. Take birth announcements, for example.

No other greeting cards—birthday, Christmas, or party invitation—generate more joy for the sender and receiver than a birth announcement. Parents select the wording and graphics that best express the excitement of the news, sometimes even creating their own.

One birth message, however, did not come inscribed on engraved parchment. What's more, it did not originate *from* the parents, but was delivered instead *to* the Nazarene mother by the angel Gabriel. "Do not be afraid, Mary, for you have found favor with God. And now, you will conceive in your womb and bear a son, and you will name him Jesus." The angel went on to report that this son would "be called the Son of the Most High and the Lord God will give to him the throne of his ancestor David." Mary was amazed. "How can this be?" She knew that she was chaste, saving herself for Joseph to whom she was engaged. Then Gabriel gave confirmation to her that the baby would be a holy child, the very Son of God. The long-awaited Messiah!

Some days later, when Mary had time to mull over the truth and cope with the glory of the angel's words, she hurried to the hills to visit her cousin Elizabeth who was also pregnant. Mary no doubt was bursting to share her secret with someone she could trust to understand. The two of them reveled in God's intended purpose. Overwhelmed by the magnitude of the event, they celebrated the promised incarnation of God. Mary was inspired to pray what is now known as the glorious Magnificat in Luke 1:46–55, in which she acknowledges her unworthiness: "My soul magnifies the Lord, and my spirit rejoices in God my Savior, for he has looked with favor on the lowliness of his servant."

This little baby, the Mighty and Holy One, would one day lift up the lowly. He would feed the hungry and be merciful to His people. What an awesome responsibility—nurturing this child, the very Son of God!

But Mary was never alone. While Mary taught Jesus human lessons in word and deed, God filled His only Son with all He was. Since Jesus was both God and man, both were needed. He referred to Himself eighty-three times in the New Testament as the Son of Man, God incarnate in flesh and holy deity, agent of divine judgment. No one had a deeper understanding of this mystery than His mother. Jesus, turning aside from His own grief and pain on the Cross, saw His grieving mother and yielded her care into the hands of John. No greater love between mother and son has been known. In the end, however, Mary's relationship to her son changed. From loving mother to child, she became faithful follower of the Son of God.

Nurturers—Giving Life

Some years ago Woman's Missionary Union secured space in five popular women's magazines in an attempt to acquaint the readers with its work. The first page of this four-page insert contained the simple message: *Giving birth is not the only miracle God gave to women.*

The second page continued: *So is giving life.*

The remaining two pages gave an account of the many ways the organization's members, including women, children, and young people, had responded to human need that year. As Christian women we attempt to both respond to the suffering and needs of others and train up our youth to do likewise. The words *mothering* and *nurturing* are often used synonymously, but giving birth is a biological event, while nurturing requires much more than the reproductive organs of a man and a woman. Jesus spoke with mothering, nurturing love when He said, "Jerusalem, Jerusalem, the city that kills the prophets and stones those who are sent to it! How often have I desired to gather your children together as a hen gathers her brood under her wings, and you were not willing!" (Matthew 23:37).

How many women have voiced that plaintive cry over their children or grandchildren? Or over others whom they have nurtured? Failures can be devastating to nurturers.

Some would say, "If nurturing is such a risky business, why get involved? I'm sure not going to set myself up for failure!" Never giving money to a beggar, they never worry about being bested by a swindler. Never expecting much out of their children, they never know sleepless nights and tear-drenched pillows. If they don't tutor a child in reading, they don't have to cry with him when he fails the mandated achievement test—again. Their advice—stay out of high crime areas and you won't get mugged.

Not long after Jesus voiced His compassion toward Jerusalem, He was killed as were the prophets before Him. When He told His disciples in a post-resurrection appearance to wait for Him in Jerusalem, they must have wondered why. Why would He ever want to acknowledge the city of such despicable acts? But immediately prior to His ascension, He cleared away all doubt. "You will receive power when the Holy Spirit has come upon you; and you will be my witnesses in *Jerusalem*" (Acts 1: 8, emphasis mine). This nurturing God never gave up on Jerusalem. Not only did the followers receive the Holy Spirit there, but they were also to launch the establishment of His worldwide church from—where else? Jerusalem! Christlike nurturers carry an invisible shield that deflects the arrows of disappointment, fear, and failure. They may be momentarily stunned, but they never give up.

Effective nurturing is probably the most important service you will ever render. Parents, grandparents, mentors, advocates—all are essential in the development of spiritually healthy persons.

Parents: First Line of Nurturers

Most nurturing occurs within the family unit. God set the pattern in the Garden of Eden. In the creation segment of *God's Trombones*, James Weldon Johnson, noted African American author, lawyer, and diplomat, gives a moving interpretation to the creation of Adam. When this great statesman drew a picture of the Creator, he used a feminine image. "Like a mammy," tenderly bending, kneeling, toiling, to create mankind.

In the minds of most, mothers are the primary nurturers of their own children. Research findings vary concerning inherent differences between the male and the female, depending on the purpose and authors of the study. But the one innate quality almost always associated with woman is nurturing. "The mother-child relationship has endured millennia of pushing and pulling with very little alteration to its essential character," Virginia Stem Owens wrote in *Daughters of Eve*. She adds, "The fact is that women routinely attend to and care for their offspring more than men, a state of affairs that has persisted for millennia."

While not all mothers are found selfless and protective of their offspring, the fact that the ideal of motherhood is still portrayed by steadfast and sacrificial love, from the time of Eve until the twenty-first century, gives credence to the nurturing factor. The numbers of single fathers providing primary care to their children is a growing but still miniscule number. Women by far carry the main responsibility in rearing the children. And most of us like it that way. Something deep within us propels us into the role. We agree with Dianne Hales' statement in her book, *Just Like a Woman:* "Becoming a mother, now and always, remains too fundamental a drive for many, even most, of us even to want to resist its pull. Regardless of our aspirations and autonomy, we hunger to give life, to feel a fetus move within our flesh, to reach, in the most tangible of ways, into the future and claim part of it as our own."

Little girls caress their dolls and borrow their own mother's expressions of love. At pre-puberty they speak of becoming mothers. Even before going into labor a mother feels emotionally connected to this embryo who was, as Psalm 139 puts it so beautifully, "being made in secret, intricately woven in the depths of the earth." How is it that parents who lose a child during pregnancy or at birth feel such a keen loss?

One young father I know, struggling to understand his deep grief when his long-awaited son was stillborn, cried out, "Why is there such hurt in losing a child we've never held, never kissed? Now I understand. In these days we've been awaiting his arrival, we've made such an emotional investment in him! He is a part of our family even though we've never really known him." While God intricately and silently weaves the child in her mother's womb, He forges an invisible bond with parents, creating a "virtual" family. At birth the bond is immediate and complete. The mother looks deep within the baby's eyes and at that moment feels complete.

After years of tenderly caring for a child's needs, love grows and the bond deepens. Do parents make mistakes? Absolutely. Do they regret the times when what they have taught in concept conflicts with what they live in example, when actions speak louder than words? Every time. Yet parents indeed are most often the primary nurturers of their offspring—and the best.

Research confirms that parents exert the most influence on teenagers, even more than their peers. A recent study in the American Journal of Sociology reports that perceived parental disapproval of premarital sex has a strong delaying factor throughout adolescence. In healthy families children strive to please their parents and avoid many pitfalls, teenage years not withstanding.

What does it take to nurture children effectively? Other than selfless love and devotion, what is the main ingredient? Investment of time is of the utmost importance. Susanna Wesley offers a hard-to-beat model for this. Susanna bore nineteen children, but nine of them died in infancy. For more than twenty years she spent six hours a day, six days a week teaching the remaining ten children. Many might wonder why she would give such a significant part of her life to the education of her children. George Stevenson recorded her words in

Memorials of the Wesley Family: "I have lived such a retired life for so many years . . . No one can, without renouncing the world in the most literal sense, observe my method. And there are few, if any, that would entirely devote above twenty years of the prime of life in hopes to save the souls of their children."

Homeschooling for Susanna demanded unusual commitment, but her investment in the lives of her children garnered much spiritual wealth, especially in the lives of sons John and Charles.

Today many women have chosen to teach their children at home in the tradition of Susanna Wesley. In early days it was a necessity where the number of schools was limited. When public schools were available everywhere in the US, some groups, including the Seventh-Day Adventists and Mormons, continued to educate their younger children at home, while the Amish kept their older children out of public schools to train them through life in the community. A new trend of homeschooling was noted in the 1970s, despite the wide availability of public schools. In the beginning of this movement, parents were pursuing a philosophy of child-led learning. Later, parents with strong religious convictions joined with the homeschool movement. While it is difficult to know for sure, it is estimated that about a half a million school-age children (approximately one percent of the total school-age population) attend school outside a school setting. Of the privately schooled population, ten percent are homeschooled.

While many states require various types of information, all state compulsory-education laws now explicitly make home schooling a valid option.

Homeschooling is not the answer for many parents, but finding quality time for interacting with children is no less important. Good parents know that the gift of time is the greatest contribution we can make to our children. My husband once asked a teenager he was counseling, "Do your parents ever talk to you?" "No," was his quick response, to which he added, "Except when I'm in trouble, and then they talk a lot!"

A father who takes an interest in car racing just to be able to communicate with his NASCAR-crazed son opens lines of communication for other topics, too. Mothers who accept the fact their daughters are turned off by cooking, sewing, or other "girl things," join enthusiastically in cheering their swimming or basketball teams. Bottom line, good parents hook in to interests of their children as a means of keeping communication open. Having points of common communion forges relationships that can weather the adversarial storms that inevitably arise.

During stormy times, parents need a strong support group—fellow strugglers and prayer warriors. Some churches facilitate such groupings, offering Christian professionals as a rich resource. Recognizing the needs parents face and meeting those needs can best be done by the church.

The church must be alert to the large number of single-mother families, as well. Aburdene and Naisbitt report in *Megatrends for Women* that in 1970, married couples headed forty percent of households in the US with children under eighteen, but in 1990 the percentage fell to twenty-six percent. Women now head twenty-nine percent of US households. One child in four, including sixty percent of black children, is now raised by a single parent. These circumstances place unbelievable stress and tension upon these mothers. The church, God's arm and heart on earth, must extend to these nurturers, giving them physical, emotional, and spiritual strength for the task that is theirs.

While it is biologically possible for irresponsible adults to give birth to a child, nurturing a child toward a productive and fulfilled life calls for genuine love and maturity. Recently newspapers across America have carried the story of the deliberate starvation of an infant by its parents. When authorities were alerted to the baby's death and were called to the home, they were shocked by what they found. A tiny, emaciated body, deprived of nourishment over time, gave some hint as to the horrific nature of the crime. The couple's only defense: drugs.

In the event parents demonstrate an inability or unwillingness to provide the proper care and nurturing of a young child, alternative parenting must be found. Adoption is often a very satisfactory means to do this.

Adoptive Parents

Flying back to the US after a trip to China, we were struck by the large number of American couples with very young Chinese babies waiting to board our plane. When curiosity got the best of us, we asked one of the young ladies if they were traveling together.

"Well, yes, and no. We aren't really a group, but all of us have come to China for the same reason, to adopt babies. Since the Chinese government has limited the number of children in a family in an attempt to control population growth, many children are sent to orphanages in hope the little ones can be adopted. It's difficult now to adopt children in the US, so we applied to adopt a Chinese baby." She pulled back the blanket for us to see her new daughter, a beautiful Asian girl with a creamy complexion and lots of shiny black hair. The mother, not an especially pretty woman, exuded a beauty reserved for those who are immensely happy and deeply satisfied. I watched as she pulled the infant to her, not breaking eye contact until the last moment before lifting her to her left shoulder, just over her own heart.

As she walked away to her husband, I was touched as he took the bundle and unashamedly kissed his daughter. It was not necessary to ask how long it would take to bond the three together. The parents shared not one gene with this new baby, were not even of the same ethnicity. They looked different in coloring, shape of nose, eyes. The baby had been born thousands of miles from the US and yet, though no one could explain how it happened, neither could anyone deny that they were a family.

No psychologist has located the source of the urgent desire by most women to have a baby. For those women who cannot bear a child, adoption, not only of Chinese babies but also of children right in our own country, melds the two in mutual need—and love.

Foster Parents
Debby Grayson, a member of my church, has opened hearth and home to foster children for several years. The first time I saw her, she was beaming over a little African American baby. It was obviously not hers. Whose was it? Every Sunday she comes holding babies in her arms or leading them by the hand. "Why?" I asked her.

"Because I feel God called me to do so. I'm a pediatric nurse and have known of the need for foster parents since seeing abused and neglected children when I practiced nursing. I wanted to help, but the time never seemed right." Debby and her husband have four children, the youngest of whom is a student in the university.

In church one Sunday morning Debby saw an item in the church bulletin reporting the need for foster parents. "I leaned over to my husband with my finger pointing the paragraph out," she recalls. "He just rolled his eyes, and I forgot it. A commitment of that magnitude necessitated agreement by both of us that it was the thing to do."

Later that week Debby received a phone call in response to her husband's request for information about foster parents. "Without my knowing it, he had made inquiry to the Department of Human Resources. I knew then that the two of us were agreed; we had to at least explore the possibility of entering the program."

Since that time, Debby and her husband have taken twelve children, some for a brief time, others for a lengthier stay. At the time of this writing two children are living in the Grayson home. Because of the confidentiality of the placements, real names of the children will not be used here. The older child (we will call him "John") was identified as an at-risk baby because of his mother's addiction to cocaine. When he tested cocaine-positive, he entered the program of Department of Human Resources, and at three months, he was placed in Debby's custody. John was the fifth child born to his African American mother. At one time, the Graysons took his two-and-a-half-year-old brother, who had been sexually abused, but because he sexually abused the other foster children, they were unable to keep him. John is a beautiful, adorable child. "He's my baby," Debby says. In two years the birth mother will have to terminate parental rights, and then

Debby hopes to adopt him.

Mindy, a second child, was born at 24 to 25 weeks gestation to a 19-year-old unwed mother. She weighed 1 pound 12 ounces. When she weighed enough, she was released from the hospital into the mother's care. But when doctors saw her again at five months, it was obvious that she was being abused. The doctor was alarmed and did further testing which revealed that Mindy was suffering from Shaken Baby Syndrome. At five months she only weighed 5 1/2 pounds. She was deaf and blind, and had cerebral edema. In addition she had reflux, and doctors suspected cerebral palsy. Social workers at the Department of Human Resources asked if Debby could take her. Because of her medical background, she was the logical one to care for this precious baby. At the time of this writing Mindy is nine months old. She has regained her hearing and sight, and she weighs 13 pounds. She has responded to love, and although she cannot sit alone, she is cooing and babbling. Her progress to this point is nothing short of a miracle.

"It's such a blessing to have these children. It's hard to say goodbye when we have to give them up. Some foster parents do adopt the children. Without question, it's the ministry to which God has called me. I'm so glad I saw that need in our church bulletin!"

More than half a million children live in foster homes, and the number is growing. The majority of them are children of color and have lived in the cities. Most have suffered trauma and have been in many living situations. While some foster children have few adjustment problems, most have suffered such neglect and abuse that they bear multiple wounds, physically and emotionally. Wendy Schwartz, in *Clearinghouse on Urban Education*, explains, "They may be aggressive in relationships as a form of self-protection, be disruptive in order to get attention, and reject others because they expect to be rejected themselves." Providing a nurturing environment for such abused children requires patience, love, and a strong sense of purpose. While adults choose to become foster parents for many reasons, they all believe they can make a difference in the lives of these children. Some have been foster children themselves or want to fill their need to be a parent. For whatever reason, they have committed to a difficult role as nurturers, but Debby says it is definitely worth the risk.

Grandmothers

The only time the word *grandmother* is mentioned in the Bible (2 Timothy 1:5), it refers to Lois, the grandmother of Timothy. Paul recognized that the young Timothy had been rooted and grounded in the faith by both his mother Eunice and his grandmother, Lois. The passage does not mention Timothy's father, but we know he was Greek and quite possibly died when Timothy was a young child. Although he was quite young when Paul first came to Lystra, Paul invited Timothy to join the group on their missionary journey. As companions, Paul became the father that Timothy had never known. Thus, the mother, grandmother and spiritual father provided the nurturing needed to encourage the spiritual gifts in Timothy's life. Who can deny the influence that Lois provided to her grandson?

Although not given the label "grandmother" in the Old Testament, what woman epitomizes the soul of a "grandmotherly" nurturer more than Naomi? You remember that most of her life story is found in the book of Ruth, because theoretically it is Ruth's story.

Naomi had been a dominant character in Ruth's life, however, from the time Ruth married Naomi's son. The closeness of the two became clear when Naomi, after the deaths of her husband and two sons, decided to leave Moab and go to her home city of Bethlehem. Ruth, although she was a Moabitess, insisted on accompanying Naomi. Naomi and Ruth had developed such a strong relationship that they were each other's primary family.

Naomi didn't simply allow the younger Ruth to take care of her when they returned to Bethlehem—she returned the favor. When Naomi discovered that her wealthy kinsman Boaz was showing special kindness to Ruth as she gleaned in his fields, she saw an opportunity for Ruth to find a home. She urged Ruth to wash, perfume, dress in her best, and go to Boaz. Boaz, impressed with Ruth, married her. In time little Obed was born, bringing joy to his parents and filling the empty arms of his grandmother Naomi.

Ruth 4:13–16 describes a most unusual and moving ceremony. The women of Bethlehem celebrated the birth of Obed, declaring their joy that Naomi had a grandson. "He (Obed) shall be to you a restorer of life and a nourisher of your old age," they declared.

Then Naomi took her grandson and held him close. "A son has been born to Naomi," the women declared, signifying a specially cherished relationship. Naomi's heart and future were full again. In the next few years she had to provide a powerful lot of nurturing, because little Obed would one day be a grandfather himself—of the great King David!

Today many grandmothers provide daily, full-time care for their grandchildren. But those of us who are only part-time caregivers fulfill significant roles in our grandchildren's nurturing as well. While we have not had our Christian friends surround us in a ritual formalizing our "grandmotherhood," perhaps we should have. The part we play in rearing a child can be significant.

When our children were grown, I thought my days of nurturing within my family were all over. Thank God, I was wrong. My role as *Bu* (Indonesian word for *Mom*) to my six grandchildren gave me a unique and precious opportunity for some of life's choicest relationships.

The Joy of Giving Life

Our children lived much of their lives as MKs, the affectionate term for missionaries' kids. Growing up so far from an extended family, missionaries form close ties with each other, creating relationships that often become closer than blood ties. The MKs called the adult missionaries "aunt" and "uncle," and a true sense of family made room for us all. Single missionaries especially had great impact on the MKs. Each year they planned and conducted a Camp MiKi for the older children. Aunt Catherine (Walker), camp director, led planning for the long-awaited event. When the children were unloaded at the campgrounds in Central Java, they never knew exactly what would happen, but it would be good. One year they observed the eruption of nearby Mount Merapi, volcano of central Java, and another year a thief entered one of the cabins by night and stole clothes. The complete trust of parents and the absolute love of the children for the camp leaders allowed the Spirit full reign during those special times. Younger children could hardly wait until they, too, were old enough to go to Camp MiKi. No one will know this side of heaven the full impact of the nurturing our children received from their missionary aunts and uncles.

Others have contributed essential elements to the lives of our three children. School and church leaders, neighbors, and family members have become special "friends," offering advice and encouragement that have expanded their horizons and challenged their directions. How grateful we are for these nurturers who have enriched their lives!

Nurturing in the Bible took many forms. Lydia led women in Philippi to pray and study by the river. When Paul came to preach Christ, he had ready-made prospects. Dorcas used her skill in sewing to clothe many in her neighborhood. Imagine the opportunities for influencing families during the fittings and modeling of finished garments. Priscilla and Aquila took a young preacher under their wings for a theological seminar in Ephesus. Apollos, an educated man, was a forceful speaker, and after Priscilla and her husband instructed him in the Scriptures, he became a powerful evangelist.

In the early church great emphasis was put on the home. The older women were to teach the younger ones to love their husbands and their children, to manage their households and to be self-controlled. (Titus 2:3–5) The weakening of the family makes this mandate even more necessary. But how do we do this? Several young ladies in my church asked that the senior women teach them how to cook "Southern." You know, grits and fried green tomatoes and okra. What a forum for teaching other things as well!

Prayer groups and Bible studies bring intergenerational groups together. Any gathering that provides maximum time for informal interaction can foster a nurturing relationship. We use gifts God has given us to model and teach—to nurture—the Christian graces.

A Woman's Role in the World

Recently while visiting in the home of a friend in Tennessee, I picked up a book entitled *Tennessee Woman: An Infinite Variety*, by Wilma Dykeman. Highlighting the achievements of women from that state, the book included a statement attributed to Anne Dallas Dudley, Tennessee leader for the ratification of the Nineteenth Amendment: "We have had a vision of a time when a woman's home will be the whole wide world, and her children all those whose feet are bare, and her sisters all those who need a helping hand."

That day has arrived. Newspapers and television reports bring needs from around the world with graphic immediacy right into our homes.

• After the world learned the fate of the victims of the 1986 Chernobyl nuclear accident, most people regretted the incident but felt helpless to do anything. While the accident resulted in 31 deaths, many more were endangered by the exposure to the radiation in the environment. A group of women from Missouri learned that getting the children out of the Chernobyl area, giving them proper nutrition and medicine for a time, could add years to their lives. They made the necessary governmental contacts, enlisted families who would receive a group of children from Belarus, and arranged for the cost of airfare. Since Missouri's experience, other groups have followed by bringing Chernobyl children to the US.

• An estimated 1.2 million children live on the streets of Russia. Another 650,000 live in orphanages maintained by the government. Children's HopeChest sponsors summer camps in Russia for Russian orphans, providing nourishing food and an opportunity to know

God's love through American missions teams.

The possibility to nurture children and women from the whole wide world is now a reality. People in our own country and from around the world cry out in need. Try as we might, we cannot muffle the sound of their suffering. Whether a woman ever bears a baby or not, she is uniquely endowed by God with the capacity to understand the pain of others, to have compassion, and to seek to relieve the hurt. Never has the need for nurturing been greater.

Urgent Need: Christian Nurturers

Most of us learned the Great Commission when we were children. "Go therefore and make disciples of all nations, baptizing them in the name of the Father and of the Son and of the Holy Spirit, and *teaching them to obey everything that I have commanded you.* And remember, I am with you always, to the end of the age" (Matthew 28:19–20, emphasis mine).

Teach them *everything*, Lord? Yes, everything. You can't do it in one sitting. To be effective, the teaching must be compelling, authentic, and demonstrated—and continued.

God has been gracious in filling us with the gifts to respond to His bidding. What's more, He has given us the supreme gift—His presence. "I am with you," not just occasionally, not just spasmodically, but always, forever and ever. Someone awaits your wisdom, experience, or maybe just your time. Teach them everything you have learned about Christ. It might take a long time.

CHAPTER 8

Aging Meaningfully

And when youth's gone
As men count going, twixt us two alone,
Still let me be Thy little child
Left learning at Thy knee.
—Anonymous

On my sixtieth birthday, my daughter Denise gave me the book *When I Am An Old Woman I Shall Wear Purple*, by Sandra Haldeman Martz. I was incensed. *An old woman?* I was just reaching the prime of life. I put the volume on the shelf next to the T-shirt with the words *Genuine Antique Person* emblazoned upon it—gift of an irreverent staff member. Whatever these dear ones were trying to tell me would just have to wait until I was beginning to consider the possibility of becoming old— some day in the distant future.

Old? How Old?

So how old are you to be *old*? Children always ask you, without a shred of shame, how old you are. I try to answer with some nonchalance something like, "Oh, about as old as dirt!" hoping to move on to another subject. But they will not be distracted, "No, how old are you really?!"

In some cultures it is permissible to ask people of all ages how old they are. While we lived in Indonesia, Annette Meriweather, the famous African American soprano, came to our city to give a series of Christian concerts. We were privileged to have her as a guest in our home. What a joy she was! Her accompanist was

Dr. T. W. Hunt, also a good friend. Her quick wit stood her in good stead when being interviewed by a young newspaper reporter:

"Miss Meriweather, how old are you?" he asked with a smile.

Annette leaned down and asked confidentially, "Can you keep a secret?"

"Oh, yes," he responded eagerly.

Again she bent down low enough to whisper in his ear, "So can I."

Women especially take pains to delay the aging process. Even young women anxiously examine their mirrored reflection for a first gray hair and the onset of a wrinkle. We buy special age-retardant creams, guaranteed to keep our complexion soft and youthful. Hair coloring replaces gray with natural brilliance. From across the whole dress department, a good eye can lock in on a dress that camouflages the bulges. For many women, "looking good" is synonymous with "looking younger."

"Down-Aging," the term coined by Faith Popcorn, describes the trend toward looking and acting younger than we are. In her book *Clicking*, she writes, "In a culture in which sixty feels like forty-five and fifty feels like thirty-five, the reality about how we live, love, work and play at a certain age is amazingly different from what we imagined or expected." As someone has said, the average life span of a woman is constantly increasing, thus enabling her to stay twenty-nine much longer. We see evidence of women pushing the age ticket daily, but why include the subject of age in a book about the timeless virtues of Christian woman?

In 1900, the average woman lived until age 49. She experienced marriage and motherhood earlier in life than today. With more children, most of whom never ventured far from home, the extended family kept her busy. Church activities and local acts of mercy made additional use of her spiritual gifts and her time. Her life, though short compared to ours, typically brought satisfaction and contentment.

Today, a century later, the average woman can expect to live to be seventy-nine. She likely has held a job at some time in her life, and married and had children. Her formal education may include one or more degrees, but her "life skills" prove as valuable. Travel and reading extend her knowledge of the world and beyond. At 65, if she is employed, she normally retires. If she is married, her husband's retirement changes their lives as well. (One friend urged my husband and me to retire at about the same time. "You need to avoid the 'two-alarm marriage' if possible.") With good health and more money than women before her, she finds some fourteen years left in her life. How she chooses to use those years can be a virtue—or a waste.

Old People in the Bible

Comments about aging in the Bible, both Old and New Testaments, are overwhelmingly positive. The elderly were to be honored and revered and appreciated for their wisdom. The children or the family of faith were to care for disabled aging persons. On the other hand, older people were admonished to be responsible and worthy examples. The aging were expected to serve God: "In old age they [the righteous] still produce fruit; they are always green and full of sap, showing that the Lord is upright; he is my rock, and there is no unrighteousness in him" (Psalm 92:14–15).

Abraham buried his beloved wife, Sarah, when she

died at age 127. She had been more than ninety when Isaac was born. Just imagine that old couple rearing a child! Sarah, although "it had ceased to be with Sarah after the manner of women" (Genesis 18:11), nursed this little miracle child.

Moses, too, exemplifies outstanding and lengthy service to God. Leading Israel out of captivity and into the Promised Land consumed his last twenty years. Nevertheless, at the age of 120 years, "his sight was unimpaired and his vigor had not abated." God led him up Mount Nebo for a view of the Israelites' destination. Moses then died on the mountain at an undisclosed location, and his people wept for him for thirty days. A truly memorable retirement occasion.

While the ages of women in the Bible are seldom revealed, we can be relatively confident they paralleled those of the men, and if true to the norm, perhaps even exceeded them slightly. We can assume also that women continued to be influential mentors and involved teachers as long as God gave them breath. Lois, notable influence in the life of Timothy, her grandson, spent her latter years in praying for and supporting him. Did Aquila precede Priscilla in death? If so, we can believe she continued alone the church planting that had been their passion into her latter years.

Psalm 90 bears the inscription, "Moses, the Man of God," the only psalm to be so designated. The honorary dedication reflects Moses' teachings and his life in general. Reflecting upon the brevity of life, the psalmist cries, "Our years come to an end like a sigh. The days of our life are seventy years, or perhaps eighty, if we are strong; even then their span is only toil and trouble; they are soon gone, and we fly away" (9–11).

Whatever the actual length of our days may be is immaterial. What we do with them is more important.

New Days for Old People

Following the devastating depression of the 1930s, President Franklin Delano Roosevelt dealt with recovery of the financial stability of the US and its people.

In 1935, Congress voted to create the Social Security Administration to assist the elderly in life needs after age sixty-five. Under Social Security, employees, their employers, and self-employed wage earners make contributions that are pooled in special trust funds. When earnings stop because of retirement, death, or disability, monthly cash benefits are paid to replace part of the earnings lost. In 1935, the life expectancy for men was 58, for women, 62 years. This rate, of course, was greatly affected by the high infant mortality, but in 1940, 9 million seniors drew Social Security payments. By 1997, life expectancy had reached 74 years for men and 79 for women. The number of Americans age 65 and up grew to 34 million.

What does all this mean? It certainly means that things are different now. Johnnie Godwin leads us carefully through the maze of retirement with his book, *Life's Best Chapter: Retirement.* He reassures retirees, "For Christians, the same One who has guided them through their earlier years is there to continue with His guidance. The pages of life's retirement chapters may be blank, but the research for further writing has largely been done. So it's time to begin."

We women are more likely to live longer, to be in better health, and to be financially better able to do what we want in our retirement years. Because women typically live longer than men, many widows face their last years alone. Those of us who enter retirement hale and hearty are not inclined to take to the rocker quite yet. Some of us may continue to work part-time. Teachers agree to substitute a stated number of days each year. Retired nurses find parish nursing brings them satisfaction. Women auditors and financial advisors are called back into duty during the tax crunch. Some women discover this is the time to do something completely different. Some even go back to school and gain new skills. What retired person has not heard, "But I thought you were retired." Instead we travel near and far, enjoy being with friends, and volunteer.

Seniors today are active, involved, and interested in helping. According to a recent survey, almost 44 percent of all people 55 and over volunteer. Over 80 percent of seniors claim membership in a religious organization like a church or synagogue. Senior volunteers find out about opportunities through their churches more than any other institutions. And it is in the church that we do much of our volunteering—teaching, serving on committees, singing in the choir, tending the little ones in the nursery, and on and on.

We carry the church with us in our hearts to teach English to a foreign student, help a child learn to read, or counsel a teenage mother. Young women need older women as mentors. A hopeless woman cries out for someone to bring purpose to her life. AIDS babies cry to be rocked, their mothers to feel acceptance. The greatest gift we can give to others is our prayers. Ask any missionary what she needs and she will nearly always answer "prayer." God's power is unleashed by prayer. We Christian women have so much to offer.

A number of years ago I read the report of a survey on volunteerism. The survey asked respondents why they volunteered hours of service or gave money to charities and agencies meeting the needs of people. One answer stood out above all the others: "because someone asked me to." It rang true in my own experience, just having walked my block collecting gifts to the Heart Association. Why? Because someone had asked me to. By asking someone to volunteer we are telling them they have something to offer. In the report mentioned above, seniors were approximately four times more likely to volunteer if they were asked. The next time you have a job to be done that requires someone with experience, expertise, and time, try asking a senior. They are a soft touch!

Never Give Up

When Timothy entered the ministry, Paul advised him, "Let no man despise your youth." Perhaps we need to be told, "Let no man despise your advanced age." Upon my retirement, I was approached about teaching a class of women my own age. In discussing the possibility with the committee, one member won me over. "We think we have ten or fifteen more years to really count for God. We want more than a Bible teacher, as important as that is. We want to be challenged to be and do all we can." My philosophy exactly! It was an offer I could not refuse. May the last of our service be the best!

In Nancy Elliott's excellent book, *Golden Opportunities: Ministry Ideas for Senior Adults*, the reader finds practical advice for using skills and energy for others. She offers dozens of ideas for involvement—an essential guide for all of us.

Wilma Weeks retired as a missionary when she was 65 years old. For more than 20 years now she has served as the chaplain in her retirement home. Laverne

Applewhite, retired missionary, went back to school to complete the certification as counselor and worked several years before retiring—again.

Recently I attended the funeral of Helen White, who for the last decade has directed an apartment ministry—after first retiring at age 65! Located directly across the street from an outstanding medical system, the residents of these apartments await donated organs for transplants. More than 14,000 have lived there for months with their families and have found emotional and spiritual support. You know of other women who defy all expectations in retirement. Choosing running shoes over house slippers, they find joy and fulfillment in serving others.

Margaret E. Burks, born in 1914, had always been the exception to the rule. She passed the Georgia CPA exam at age 39 and graduated magna cum laude from University of Georgia two years later. She married Jesse Burks, 20 years older than she, and when he retired they moved to Florida. She loved working in her church with all the missions organizations. When Jesse died, Margaret made her first missions trip to Monrovia, Liberia, West Africa, in 1985. She served as Bible teacher, swimming instructor, and crafts director for a girls camp. She was hooked! In the next six years, she made nine other missions trips to Liberia to help construct eight church buildings.

At age 76, Margaret felt led to go to back to school. In 1996, at the age of 81, she was graduated from New Orleans Baptist Theological Seminary with a Master of Divinity Degree in Pastoral Ministries—at the top of her class. Just four months later, Margaret went to Arusha, Tanzania, to teach Old Testament in the International Baptist Theological Seminary of East

Africa. In addition, she served as manager of the bookstore, treasurer of her church, and director of the women and children's divisions of the seminary.

Summing up her service for the Lord in Africa, she says, "I am glad God does not put us on the shelf when we reach the age of 55, 65, 75, or even 85! To God be the glory, great things He has done!"

Researchers would have great difficulty finding exact numbers of seniors who take volunteer assignments to minister overseas. They fill places on missions teams in their churches and build houses for Habitat for Humanity. Universities call on them for teaching English and other professional assignments. Doctors fill in for medical missionaries to attend meetings or serve temporarily in another place. While they meet their official job responsibilities, seniors serve as surrogate grandparents as well. Our little three-year-old daughter climbed uninvited into the lap of our eldest missionary the first time she saw him. We had only been in Indonesia a few months, and she missed her grandparents.

Not all courageous seniors go overseas. Ada Jennings and three other elderly members had seen their Texas church's membership virtually disappear by 1993. At their request a larger church agreed to sponsor them as a mission. The mother church sent a retired pastor who quickly got caught up in the dream. For several years they served the church, and gradually people began to come.

Hanging on the walls of the thriving Oran Baptist Church today are certificates testifying to the church's missions giving and their growth in Sunday School. The pastor reports, "It is unbelievable what God has done for this little church. We come to church every

Sunday to see what God is going to do." Two of the four elderly women who would not let the church die are deceased; one is in assisted living. The fourth? She is now an "honorary trustee at age ninety-four, and still believes in the future of Oran Church."

Billy Graham and his wife, Ruth, epitomize the title "Faithful Servant" to people around the globe. Evangelists have risen and fallen around this godly man. Not once has he failed to live the message he so effectively proclaims. Dr. Graham is now in his 80s and suffers from Parkinson's disease. Yet he is looking forward to evangelistic crusade opportunities. Mrs. Graham is in a wheelchair after five hip replacement procedures. Her assessment of her condition? A recent interviewer discovered Mrs. Graham has a "Don't ask, don't tell" policy about her health. She did have advice for those who are in constant pain and anguish. "Get your mind off yourself and on other people." The interviewer, Ken Garfield, closes with this poignant statement: "I'll choose to remember the Grahams well past their prime—how a faltering preacher and his ailing wife refused to let doctors and wheelchairs keep them from delivering a message that goes well beyond Christianity. This message is one that people of all faiths and even no faith can embrace: Never give up."

We women of America have been blessed by extended years and adequate resources for continuing ministry past retirement. We would be unwise to ignore the voices that warn against depleting the Social Security funds for future generations. With the expanding numbers of the elderly, especially as the baby boomers mature, we face the reality of unfunded liability of retirement programs. Seniors of the future will possibly work past the age of sixty-five and live on smaller retirement incomes. But never again will we believe a date on the calendar determines when life is over. Aging is a process, not an event.

When the Voice Is Stilled

Kate O'Brien, my husband's mother, could preach the stars down. Oh, she would have denied the title "preacher," but anyone who heard her was moved by her passionate proclamation of the Word. She loved the Bible and spent hours each day drinking in its truths. She taught in churches, community centers, large auditoriums, and in her home. Women of all ages flocked to hear her teach. When she was in her late 80s, her health began to decline. No longer was she able to stand and teach before groups. But still she could speak to individuals and encourage them in their walk of faith. And then small strokes robbed her of her ability to speak. How sad to be with her but not have the benefit of her wisdom and experience! Perhaps even then, however, her prayers of intercession for us and others continued to ascend to the Father.

All of us will experience the diminishing of abilities required for active service for our Lord. Jesus instructed His disciples to "work the works of him who sent me while it is day; night is coming when no one can work" (John 9:4). Although His voice was momentarily stilled by Calvary, His ministry continued in the lives of those who followed Him. Our active ministry will ultimately slow and finally end. The "minister to" becomes the "ministered unto."

My own mother was confined to her bed in her final days. How she looked forward to visitors! Ladies from a local church brought her flowers that never failed to cheer her up. When I visited her, she always said, "You talk." Formulating words of her own was difficult, but she hungered for news of others. When we asked her to pray for specific things, she always wanted to know the outcome.

We must not forget our elders who are living in their last days. Their needs are many and range from assistance in managing their financial affairs to talking about the process of dying. They love singing, jokes, and little children. Reading Bible passages and having a brief prayer are frequently requested. Touching them—holding their hands, rubbing their hands with lotion, and brushing their hair—has a calming effect. One of my friends, a retired nurse, came regularly and gave Mother pedicures. If possible, take them outside in a wheelchair on a pretty day. In short, don't forget them. Visits should not be long; they tire easily. Caregivers need a rest and appreciate being given the opportunity to be away for even a short while.

"Growing old is not for weaklings," is often said with a grin. It's not to be done alone, either. Our elders need us. If God has given you this ministry, you are especially blessed. When life is diminished by poor health and failing senses, your touch and smile says, "You are still loved and appreciated." It's a gift from God.

Grow Old Along with Me

"So teach us to count our days, that we may gain a wise heart" (Psalm 90:12 NRSV).

"Teach us to use wisely all the time we have" (Psalm 90:12 CEV).

Some people would like to skip past the last years of life. Recently I heard of a woman complaining about God not letting her die. She was ready to go, but God would not hear her prayers.

A sympathetic friend offered, "Maybe He still has something He wants you to do." Indignantly, she resolutely squared her shoulders and avowed, "Well, I'm not going to do it!"

The teacher in Ecclesiastes offers a grim metaphor of old age in chapter 12. The physical body fails us; we lose the ability to see and hear. No longer can we depend on agility and dexterity. The white-haired woman fears heights and terror. And then the fragile silver cord is broken. Grim.

Robert Browning gives a more favorable report in his poem "Rabbi Ben Ezra":

> Grow old along with me!
> The best is yet to be,
> The last of life, for which the first was made:
> Our times are in his hand,
> Who saith, "A whole I planned,
> Youth shows but half; trust God: see all, nor be afraid."

God is allowing us to have more years than ever before in a lifespan. You may be so young that old age seems eons away. One day you will say, "It seems like only yesterday . . ." Others of you have lived most of your life, and fear having the rest pass too quickly. The prayer for all of us is that God will teach us to use wisely all the days we have.

Once we put our hand to the plow in active service for our Lord. One day, try as we may to delay it, we will lose our grip. The work assigned to us will be passed on to another, not because we have been negligent or unfaithful. No, no. We will be promoted to an even greater responsibility in the kingdom prepared for us by the Lord Jesus himself.

By the way, I have slipped the book off the shelf—you know, the one I mentioned at the beginning of this chapter. Quite interesting. I have also started wearing the sweatshirt, the Genuine Antique one. It looks great with my jeans!

CHAPTER 9
Connecting Across Cyber-Fences

Two women worked their vegetable gardens in adjacent backyards. Each of the two areas gave proof of the owner's love of nature and hours of toil. Though it was still early spring, grass and shrubs were trimmed and fertilized for the growing season. The two women were preparing the sections that later would be the summer garden. They had turned the soil, put lime and fertilizer down as they had done for several years. The cyclone fence that separated the adjacent areas did nothing to divide the two friends. In fact, they had deliberately chosen these areas so that they could visit while gardening.

"Martha, do you remember Nancy, who used to live down the street?"

"You mean the one who was going to Japan to do missionary work?"

"Yes, well, she told me this morning that her husband was in a car accident near Osaka and was hospitalized."

"How terrible! When did it happen?"

"This morning. She was calling from the emergency room. She wanted me to let the five hundred people all over the world who receive their newsletter know as soon as possible so they could pray."

"How in the world are you going to do that? Telephone calls to that many people would cost a fortune."

"Indeed it would. And it would take forever to reach them all. Instead I typed out a message on my computer and sent it by email to the list already set up for their newsletter. One stroke of the 'send' button, and the message is on its way. Nancy will send me an update each day that I will then pass on to the prayer partners. That way everyone will know exactly how to pray."

"That's awesome! A few years ago, that would not have been possible. Could we pray for them right now?"

Actually, that conversation never took place. I remember very well, however, the many times my friend Martha and I visited across the backyard fence. Martha was a school librarian, so we shared many interests as well as a summer vacation. Her garden enticed me into trying my hand as well. The digging and weeding always seemed to give ample time to talk about whatever was of interest to us. I guess neighbors have been visiting across backyard fences for a long time.

But today the fences have opened out to make the whole world our backyard. People and information once far from us are now as accessible as next door. Backyard fences have become cyber-fences through the amazing capabilities of the Internet. Computers, once far too expensive for home use, now come with price tags reasonable enough for the average family. The computer operations are simple enough to be "user-friendly" and difficult enough to be "user-frustrating" from time to time. Before giving up on it entirely, you can always call in an expert—the high school kid in your neighborhood.

When talk first started about the day when computers would be used in the classroom, I was skeptical. To those who predicted that the computer would revolutionize learning, I had one response: "Just another teaching machine that will end up in the closet. Computers won't make any more difference ultimately than other fads in education have." Was I ever wrong!

Just a semester later I was enrolled in a computer class at Virginia Commonwealth University in Richmond. We used punch cards to enter the data into a computer so large that it was housed in a separate building. After entering our data, we then hovered over an enormous printer that would eventually spit out the results we requested. Toward the end of the semester when final reports were due, the crowd around the computer grew, all waiting patiently (or not) for the printout of their project solution to appear. Mistakes in the data entry in the program my class studied resulted in a brief message on the final report. Back to the drawing board. The consequences of errors in another program, however, were much more dramatic. The printer in that case delivered pages and pages of indecipherable letters and numbers. Adding insult to injury, at the bottom of each page were the words *Postmortem Dump*.

That computer course did not qualify for Most Interesting Course, at least in my book. I never became competent in programming in my "language," Cobalt, because I really didn't get it. However, on my way to class each day, I passed students sitting in front of screens and typing on typewriters. Someone said they were PCs, personal computers. When computers finally made it to the classroom, they were in the form of PCs, and I soon came under their spell.

Women with Connections
The "virtuous woman" of Proverbs 31 was commended for her business expertise. She was equally effective in her parenting and homemaking responsibilities. Each

facet of her life required networking and connecting with other people. Through negotiation with business owners, she was able to buy and sell wool and negotiate for the purchase of a field. Though her merchandise was of the highest quality, she could not make a profit without reaching a deal with a buyer. Especially in her ministry to the poor it was necessary that she give verbal expression of her compassion.

Communication has always been the glue that bound individuals together. Women especially seek "togetherness" with others. Networking and connecting come naturally to us.

The desire and ability to communicate with others signals emotional health and intellectual development in the human. Adam and Eve conversed with God in the Garden of Eden. Remember? "God commanded them, 'You may freely eat of every tree in the garden, but . . .'" Too bad they didn't remember. Language has always been important.

The Word Goes Out

Our Proverbs 31 woman, representing entrepreneurial women down through the ages, would shake her head in disbelief at the speed of change in communication in the past century. When the virtuous woman needed to send a message to someone far away, she employed a courier to deliver it.

Would the Proverbs superwoman be involved in the computer flurry of today? You bet! Could we, virtuous women of today, find uses enough to propel us into cyberspace? As methods that claim to increase the capacity to communicate have materialized, we have to evaluate and analyze the potential in our own lives. It may be that an invaluable resource lies at our fingertips.

Women in the Internet Flow

It took thirty-eight years for commercial radio to reach an audience of 50 million, thirteen years for television, but only five years for the Internet to have that many users. The US leads the world in home Internet use, with more than 98 million people logging on from home in December 2000. Lower costs for PCs and free Internet access have enabled many average earners to log on.

In addition the study reported that more women were online than men (51.1 percent). What's more, according to another study, thirty-three percent of online US households have had access for less than a year. Sixty percent of these are women and many earn average and below-average incomes.

What do these Internet users find to do on the Web? Email was at the top of the list for 68 percent of those polled. Email is fast becoming the communication tool of choice for US adults. Men are more likely to open their business emails first, but—guess what—women open their personal mail first. Are you surprised?

Searching for information took second place for women in the survey of Internet use. Students today head first for their computers instead of the library when attacking a research paper. The information online is easily accessible and up-to-date. As for any citation, considering the reliability of the source is especially important on the Internet.

For me, searching online is like entering a candy shop. I am amazed at the abundance of information. Once I had heard the phrase "women holding up half the sky," I was intrigued. What was its source? Who originally said it? Not knowing where to look on the Internet, I simply did a search on the phrase itself.

Within a few seconds I learned it came from Mao Tse-tung's *Little Red Book*, and referred to the importance of women in the Communist revolution.

Many regular Internet users say that the Net has significantly changed their lives. But there are those who believe that the Internet is an "isolating technology" that could have serious repercussions on the social fabric of communities as users interact less with other people. Others are concerned about a potentially harmful effect on the morality of the users and fear it is a threat to family life. A study released by the Pew Internet and American Life project in May 2001 found that more than half of the American adults who don't use the Internet have little or no desire to get online. Fear, technophobia, and lack of interest are among the main reasons. Generally, however, most people believe that in time, aversion to the Internet will disappear. After all, most new technologies are met with some manner of fear and resistance. So before we rush headlong into a decision to be Internet-less, let's examine the positive things the Internet offers women.

Women on Board

We have already mentioned that women make use of the Internet for email more than any other purpose. We can actually exchange messages with friends around the world with little or no knowledge of other computer functions. In fact, less expensive equipment can be purchased for emailing exclusively.

Since my son Ross has a computer business, he considered it a part of his boys' education to become computer-literate as soon as possible. So, he got email addresses for each of them when they were four and two years old. When Connor, the four-year-old, was in kindergarten, he caught the chicken pox and had to stay home from school for a few days. Wanting him to know we were thinking of him, I sent him an email greeting. When he awakened that morning, he noticed the computer was on, so he decided to check his mail. He logged on to the Internet and accessed the Web site where he got his mail. He then entered his name and password and saw he had one message. He clicked on the message notification, and my greeting came up on the screen. There was just one problem—he couldn't read it! Children have no inhibitions about or fears of the computer. Too bad we were born twenty years too soon.

Women have additional uses for the Internet. Gleaning information for many different reasons, we find the gold mine of data mind-boggling. We can find a wealth of information about medical diagnoses that have been made and the medicines prescribed to cure them. Travel information—maps, tourist sites, weather forecasts—almost anything one might want to know for a trip can be found on the Internet. Newspapers and magazines from all over the world can be accessed. Shopping for clothes, books, appliances, and most anything you would want to buy can be expedited over the Internet. Many even bank and pay bills on line. E-Business is big in today's world.

Women who want to complete college degrees can preview Web sites of colleges and universities in the US and other countries as well. All course requirements can be met online. A friend of mine recently completed a Master's degree in computer technology and took every class at home, behind her computer. No wonder a growing number of women take advantage of this amazing new tool.

The Internet has some unsavory users as well. In January 2001, the *Chicago Tribune* carried an article entitled "Prostitutes hook up to the net." In it the reader learned that prostitutes in Rio de Janeiro, Brazil, were soliciting customers on the Internet. Other sites, the article also informs us, are being used by criminals to exploit women who have been forced or tricked into prostitution. While sex trafficking has been known in certain parts of the world for many years, the Internet makes its marketing possible around the world.

Shortly after reading this article, I was looking at a list of personnel requests from a mission board. Imagine my surprise to find a request for a minister/counselor for the sex industry in Brazil! It seems to be a timely appeal for Christians wanting to make a difference in a new day.

Moms on Guard

US college seniors are the most wired group in the US, according to a recent study. Virtually all of them use the Internet. Nine out of ten use email daily, but only thirteen percent send handwritten letters. Four out of five get their news and information online, while a little over fifty percent turn to radio or TV. These young adults spend an average of eleven hours a week on the Internet, almost twice as much as they did as freshmen.

Seventy-three percent of America's teenagers, about 17 million of them, are online, according to a Pew Internet project. These teens believe their use of the Internet plays a major role in their relationships with their friends, their families, and their schools. However, a majority of them think it takes away from the time young people spend with their families.

Computer education may begin in preschool, but

certainly by kindergarten school systems make provisions for PCs and instruction in order to stay current in today's education. Children normally take to the computer like fish to water, while we adults are like calves looking at a new gate. When we were young, we obediently waited for someone to teach us how to use a new tool before we touched it. Not today's youth. With neither hesitation nor fear they move in to push, pull, and slide every moving part. How do they develop computer skills so quickly? They learn by doing. If one key doesn't work, they just try another until they figure it out themselves. They fearlessly approach the technology as something to conquer. One teacher decided to offer computer classes for his students' parents. In commending them for their progress, he said, "You're doing great—almost as well as my fourth graders!"

With this acquired skill, our youth are better equipped for life. Unfortunately, however, they also are placed in very vulnerable positions. Since few parameters are placed on Internet content, every possible subject and influence is there for the taking.

On one hand, moms agree that the Internet is a good educational tool for their children and that it is a good resource for finding answers to questions they have about parenting. However, most parents believe that their children's use of the Internet should be monitored. They also generally agree that children's time online should be limited. Most would also agree that the filtering out of sites dangerous to children is necessary. But should parents spy on their children? Absolutely, say most. Keeping track of your child's activity online or off isn't spying, it's good parenting. Little children are monitored constantly, but as they get older they receive more freedom and more privacy. Privacy becomes a more difficult issue when the child becomes a teenager, but good parents still retain responsibility for their well being and keeping them from harm's way. Parents who close their eyes and hope for the best are simply abdicating this responsibility and leaving their children vulnerable to evil and smut online.

Parents need to know the dangers and risks children encounter on the Internet. They most fear the sexually explicit material, and with good cause. Without some filtering device, children will likely stumble on X-rated material. Innocent children and youth easily access sites portraying violence and advocating harmful acts toward others, especially of other racial or religious groups. They can find sites advocating profanity, suggesting suicide, giving recipes for making bombs, offering satanic cults, and on and on. They can buy or sell drugs and even gamble online. The Internet can be a frightening experience.

But the most dangerous aspect of the Internet is not pornography or email, but chat rooms. Someone has described the general chatroom as being like a street corner in New Orleans during Mardi Gras or a New Year's Eve at Times Square. Ordinary people are there along with con artists and dangerous predators. And everyone is anonymous. The conversations often center around sex and other topics unsuitable for children. Predators lure innocent children to meet them with the intention of doing them harm. Not being able to interpret the intent, unknowing minors have experienced serious assaults as a result. According to a study published in 2001 in the Journal of the American Medical Association, one in five young people who used the Internet at least once a month in 2000 received unwanted sexual solicitations. Only ten percent of the incidents were reported to police, school officials, or an Internet service provider. The report recommended impressing upon youngsters the importance of filing complaints.

These warnings are not meant to urge you to bar your child from the Internet, but to supervise your child's use of it. When properly monitored, the Internet offers her or him a whole new world of wholesome fun and learning. Twelve million children are now online, and the number will keep growing. Proper use of the Internet may increase a student's school performance and job potential. Because it can also present unsafe situations, parental guidance and supervision are necessary. Know your child's email account and password to make periodic checks possible. Keep the lines of communication open regarding people they chat with, and report any unwanted mail to your Internet provider. An Internet filtering service will provide other protective practices as well. In summary, the following tips are good enough to remember and to pass on:

• Establish clear ground rules for Internet use.
• Place your computer in the family room or another open area of your home.
• Spend time with your children on the Internet pointing out (and learning about) interesting and helpful sites.
• Teach your children never to give out their personal information to people they have met online, especially in chat rooms or bulletin boards.
• Instruct your child never to plan a face-to-face meeting alone with an online acquaintance.
• Tell your child not to respond when they receive offensive or dangerous email or chat communications, but to tell you.

The Internet is a powerful resource, and power always has the potential for good and evil. We dare not disregard either.

The Online Church

It takes time to adapt to a new medium. Take television, for example. Expanding out of radio, TV programming predictably borrowed from the "talking head" method of radio. As time passed, producers and directors explored the capacities of television and developed new and more appealing techniques. When we rent an old movie, we find the slow pace boring after the action and effects to which we have been accustomed.

Computer programming has gradually expanded to new levels, too, as we have seen its applicability in every area. Imagine a current Web site that includes all these:

• Scripture verse for the day and comment of the week
• Review of current events with religious significance
• Bookstore for faith studies
• Addresses and times of nearby worship services
• Prayertimes
• Multimedia presentations
• Schedule of tours to religious sites
• Business and financial assistance
• Spiritual help for alcoholics
• And much more.

The Internet address of this Web site? Would you believe www.islam.org?

When Christian churches first began building Web sites, they were unaware of the infinite capacities of this medium. The Webmaster dutifully logged in information needed to locate the church building, times of worship, and a list of the church staff. Sometimes a sermon or Bible study would be included. Today one out of three Protestant churches has a Web site, and many are planning one in the future, according to Barna Research Online. This study found that the content of church Web sites varies tremendously. Most include scheduled activities, information about the church, and current church news. Only a small margin went beyond these basics.

Barna's study also included the place of the Internet in people's spiritual lives, and reports that "within this decade as many as 50 million individuals may rely solely upon the Internet to provide all of their faith-based experiences." They predict from the information gathered that these people will be "listening to religious teaching, reading online devotionals, and buying religious products online."

If these predictions are accurate, Christian churches need to expand their Net-based options. Otherwise, the resources found on www.islam.org, along with those of every religion known to man will be there offering to feed their souls.

In 312 B.C., the Appian Way was built, the first of the system of Roman highways. By the time Rome was at its greatest strength, it had built fifty thousand miles of highway across which merchants, traders, teachers, governmental entourages, and others passed. Paul no doubt frequented this road. The Bible tells us that in the "fullness of time" the Messiah came. Was this provision of a means to transport the good news a part of the "fullness of time"? The Roman highway was neither holy nor even "religious," but it was a means to get the gospel before larger and more diverse audiences. The Internet serves that same purpose for us today.

When churches recognize the possibilities the

Internet offers churches in reaching people who are hidden away, we will gladly invest the financial resources needed for an effective Web site. By providing Bible studies and discipleship classes online, many who would never darken the door of the church will hear the Word. Chat rooms provide the needed anonymity for some who need it to discuss spiritual matters. On topics such as alcoholism, homosexuality, AIDS, and teenage pregnancy, people could find the help some would be unable to seek otherwise. Devotionals, movie and book reviews, resources for worship and Christian music could be the options that bring people back— and possibly into—the local church.

Barna makes a startling prediction. He states that by the end of the decade, more than ten percent of our population will rely on the Internet for their entire spiritual experience. Some will be people who have never been church members before, but millions will be people who drop out of the physical church in favor of the "cyberchurch." The study also states that almost all the faith community will be influenced by online faith developments.

Many of you are way beyond the curve. You long since have learned the joys and pains of surfing the Internet and of hearing those happy words, "You've got mail." Just maybe, however, you are still not convinced that a computer is the best thing since sliced bread and wonder what place it has in the life of a Christian woman. Can it enrich my spiritual life?

Christian Women Connecting
We have already seen the many ways the Internet can be used to grow and serve Christ. Your church Web site needs many people to keep the material up-to-date,

inviting, and compelling. You may be called to write a devotional, lead a chat room discussion, or review a book online. Missions reports may be your contribution. On the other hand, you may need to be the one who champions the cause for having a Web site.

In addition, you may be interested in using your computer for personal Bible study. Your Christian bookstore has commentaries, Bible dictionaries, atlases, and other helps on CD-ROM. Religious music can be a help in your meditation or when you are working online.

Having prayer groups or Bible study groups online in chat rooms is possible in all kinds of weather. Sunday School class meetings or committee meetings online cut commuting time out for busy women.

But perhaps the most popular function of the Internet is email. Use it for prayer opportunities— updating requests, sending late-breaking news, sharing the joy of answers. Connect with missionaries through email to get their newsletters online, and to provide your support through prayer. Email friends and those you mentor to offer encouragement and just to say you love them and are praying for them.

At present we have a dear friend in a distant city who is very ill. Each day someone I do not know personally sends an email about my sick friend. I am only one on a network of many people who have special interest in her. To telephone each one of us would be impossible because of time and expense. But through email time and expense are minimal. And the blessings are large!

I keep thinking about Paul, trudging along the road or looking out over the rail of a ship, perhaps thinking how fortunate he was to have been born in such an advanced age.

If he had been born in Abraham's day, travel would have been much more difficult, following the paths of animals through the hills and valleys. But in Paul's time the roads provided smooth passage for the most part, and towns and cities were a source for lodging and buying a little food. He no doubt thought much about friends along the way—Priscilla and Aquila, Timothy—others whom he loved. And the churches—how he must have prayed for them as he traveled! Paul was a connector of individuals and of churches. He did so much in his day under what seems to us to have been primitive circumstances. What would he have done with the many tools God has given us?

God has placed within women that same capacity for caring and reaching out to others. He has provided the message and the means. Now we are the connectors, reaching across barriers, to the unreached ones, to those who do not know Jesus. May we be as faithful with the many technological miracles of our day as others in the past have been without them.

CHAPTER 10
Being a Lifelong Learner

Education has always been important—but education was not always considered important for women. When our nation was formed, only the very wealthy or highly intelligent or unusually progressive educated their daughters. A tutor normally provided private instruction for the girl fortunate enough to receive it. The subject matter usually included classical and domestic subjects. Thankfully, our national leaders realized in time that everyone profited by the ability to read and write and to do computation. Therefore, they founded public schools to provide free education for all children.

By the 1930s the normal age to begin school was six. It was hoped that the children would learn to read during that first grade. Any child who did not would be retained until she or he could. Some children dropped out because they were not "smart enough," or because they were needed by the family to help put bread on the table.

American students today spend more time in a classroom than ever before. They begin school at an earlier age and many have an expanded school year. Education is a priority for parents, taxpayers, and governmental leaders, yet it seems we still have not found the formula for adequately developing the minds of our youth. Some still drop out of school, and a percentage lack the incentive to invest the effort and time to become real students. However, the good news is that more women than ever go on to study in a college or university, equipping themselves for professional positions with bachelor's and advanced degrees. Older women who were unable to go to college after high school sit side by side in class with much-younger women. New programs are offered especially for women. The women's studies program offered in many universities today includes courses and content distasteful to many Christian women, but other options are being developed. The Christian Women's Leadership Center at Samford University is a good example. A woman can take individual courses for credit or noncredit, intending to upgrade her leadership skills in church or ministry and professional areas. Others opt to take a core program of Christian women's studies and finish out a master's degree with classes in another graduate area.

Women in the workplace typically find that jobs change and require new skills. Computerization in almost every arena is a notable example. Some jobs, such as teaching, require ongoing training. Formal education seems to go on forever for some—the professional students.

But many of us continue to be learners without ever stepping a foot into a school building or paying a cent for tuition. We continue throughout life to build on our body of knowledge, both to satisfy our own curiosity and to enhance our ability to serve others. While our bodies at some point in life stop growing, our minds have the potential for expansion throughout life. In fact, scientists tell us that an active, healthy mind keeps us younger. So if you want to stay young, keep up your learning program. It's a wonderful age retardant!

What are the requirements for becoming a life-long learner? What does it take to keep our minds alert and our lives productive?

First, *you need an insatiable curiosity.* It's easy to cruise through the day in neutral, our minds totally disengaged. I worried about our daughter walking home from school when she was in first grade. It wasn't very far, but it seemed to take her a long time. So I watched her. She noticed a pretty stone and picked it up to see the colors at closer range. She saw a toad jumping out of the yard nearby and watched to see how those "kicker" legs worked.

An airplane broke the sound barrier, and she patiently waited until the trail of white gradually faded in the sky. Where did we lose the wonder of it all? How can we miss the enchantment of the ordinary?

Not every subject turns everybody on to learning. One professor offered, "If you have any intelligence, you will want to know how an airplane flies." I listened to that quote several times and finally gave myself permission to disagree. Obviously, *someone* should care, but the rest of us can put our attention on other subjects of importance.

Formerly, intelligence tests that assessed our knowledge of facts reputedly quantified our IQ. Persons whose IQ scores were higher were expected to be better students and more successful. Not so. Many with high IQs had less-than-stellar career paths, while marginal students often became very successful. Other kinds of intelligence figured into accomplishment for many people. Skill in interpersonal relationships, in aesthetics, in leadership, and other identifiable areas had to be factored into the mix also. Learning is much more complicated than educational psychologists thought.

What turns you on to learning? Laboratories for learning surround us—libraries, museums, the Internet. But don't forget personal observation, experimentation, and conversation with other learners, and—you name it! Satisfy your curiosity.

Keep an open mind. Michael Michalko in his book, *Thinkertoys*, offers exciting exercises in creativity, because "By changing your perspective, you expand your possibilities until you see something that you were unable to see before." When we refuse to consider new options and hold preconceived ideas too closely, we miss some of life's best truths.

A little girl just beginning to dress herself would often get her shirt on backwards. Her mother patiently and repeatedly told her that the label should always be in the back. One day the mother found her in her closet busily occupied cutting the labels out of her shirts. When her mother asked her why, the little girl said, "I didn't want to know which was the back."

Be intentional about learning. After we have finished our formal education, some of us think learning is all over. We are surprised to learn that our best days for adding to our knowledge are ahead. It was by chance that I discovered that truth most clearly.

When we lived in Indonesia and the children were little, I homeschooled them. I had never enjoyed social studies when I was a girl, but in order not to poison the children with my distaste for the topic, I tried to find different ways to present the material. The year before we were to return to the US, Erin's social studies entailed a survey of world geography. Since we planned to take a brief tour through Europe on our way home, Erin and I planned our itinerary through the social studies for the year. What would have normally been a memorable trip for both of us became even more worthwhile because our studies together had purpose and intention.

Why is it so important for us to continue learning all our lives? For starters, an increased knowledge of God's world and its peoples gives us a deeper understanding of the measure of His love for us all. The endless variety of His creation generates awe in its beholders. Study broadens our appreciation of all God has given us.

Continuous learning keeps us from making the mistakes others have made before us. As early as the first century B.C. it was said, "From the error of others a wise man corrects his own." And a wise woman.

Keeping up with current events makes us wiser and more responsible citizens. Awareness of need is the first step in becoming obedient in a ministry. A well-rounded woman has a wealth of options in approaching another woman about spiritual matters. God has equipped us with multiple senses for gathering information for use on His behalf. We dare not be lazy and indifferent to His many gifts.

Our greatest challenge as Christian women, however, is to continue to grow in our knowledge of Christ—to become more like Him every day.

Knowing God

Our granddaughter Kristen never meets a stranger. She loves people of all ages. Everyone she meets is her newest best friend. Entering a room, her internal radar directs her to an unfamiliar face and she launches in with conversation. "Hi. What's your name? Do you live near here? That's a pretty dress." Her father, a pastor, calls her his walking Rolodex. If he forgets the identity of one of his parishioners, he can always ask Kristen. Not only will she supply the name he seeks, but she can also provide the names of other family members, where they live, and sometimes their telephone numbers. All attempts to warn her of the danger of speaking to people she doesn't know falls on her deaf ears.

We may not be as facile as Kristen about names but knowing someone's name is only the beginning of knowing them. Our eyes process the visual and auditory stimuli—the shape of their bodies, color of hair, tone of their voices—and we call their names. My husband was picking up some things at the grocery store recently and saw our neighbor, Lane, from across the street. Bill called his name and tried to engage him in conversation. Strangely, he never responded beyond a slight nod. Bill was puzzled, until he remembered one fact. Lane had an identical twin! Bill had just met him.

The physical characteristics of a person are helpful in making identification, but getting inside the skin of another is quite another thing. We may think we can predict what our husbands or close friends will do, but even those closest to us sometimes surprise us.

If we feel incompetent in truly knowing our friends and family members whom we can see and hear and touch, how can we possibly know God? No one has ever seen Him. He is infinite and unseen. Philip Yancey quotes an ancient Orthodox writer in *Reaching for the Invisible God:* "God cannot be grasped by the mind. If He could be grasped, He would not be God." He then adds, "We are profoundly different, God and I, which explains why friendship is not the primary model used in the Bible to describe our relationship. Worship is." If we cannot see Him, how can we be like Him?

Seeking the Mind of God

As good students, we seek *information*, but more is required of us as good *disciples*. The dictionary meaning of disciple is one who receives instruction from another.

Dallas Willard, in *The Divine Conspiracy*, says, "A disciple, or apprentice, is simply someone who has decided to be with another person, under appropriate conditions, in order to be capable of doing what that person does or to become what that person is." As true disciples, we seek the heart of God. Neglecting to take this all-important step, we Christians are too often misled in purpose, misguided in direction, and, as a result, forfeit the power of His Spirit and the joy of His presence.

When Moses was readying the Israelites to enter the Promised Land, God provided the heart of the orientation. Deuteronomy 29 clarifies His covenant with the people, an addition to the covenant He had made with them earlier in Horeb. Moses, God's servant leader in the exit from Egypt, knew his tenure was coming to an end. He above all knew the weaknesses and foibles of the Israelites. The image of the golden calf was engraved upon his mind.

In Deuteronomy 29:2–4 Moses makes the following observation: "You have seen all that the Lord did before your eyes in the land of Egypt, to Pharaoh and to all his servants and to all his lands, the great trials that your eyes saw, the signs, and those great wonders. *But to this day the Lord has not given you a mind to understand, or eyes to see, or ears to hear*" (emphasis mine).

After all the years in the wilderness, the Israelites lacked the mind of God to understand His involvement in their lives and in the lives of their fellow Israelites. Imagine the quick defense of the chastised Israelites. "How can we understand the thoughts and intents of God? Who can know his thoughts? He is the Holy God."

Centuries later, Paul asks this very question in his letter to the Corinthians: "For what human being knows what is truly human except the human spirit that is within? So also *no one comprehends what is truly God's except the Spirit of God*" (1 Corinthians 2:11, emphasis mine).

The Israelites knew nothing of the form of God. As members of God's chosen people, they had limited experience with God's Spirit, who made His presence and power known primarily through Moses. For the church in Corinth, however, Paul brings a new and different message in verses 12 and 13: "Now we have received not the spirit of the world, but the Spirit that is from God, so that we may understand the gifts bestowed on us by God. And we speak of these things in words not taught by human wisdom *but taught by the Spirit, interpreting spiritual things to those who are spiritual*" (emphasis mine).

Not only are God's people urged to seek the mind of Christ, we are told in 1 Corinthians 2:16: "'For who has known the mind of the Lord so as to instruct him?' But *we have the mind of Christ*" (emphasis mine). We have the mind of Christ. *The Message* interprets the passage this way: "Isaiah's question, 'Is there anyone around who knows God's Spirit, anyone who knows what he is doing?' has been answered: Christ knows, and we have Christ's Spirit."

Why did the people of Old Testament days not have full discernment of the heart of God while the Corinthians and all other believers since have found access even to the mind of Christ? It had to do with the fullness of time (Hebrews 1); because it was God's plan to send Jesus to the world to show us how to live and then send the Spirit to indwell us and appropriate His power and interpret His mind. "Long ago God spoke to our ancestors in many and various ways by the prophets, but in these last days he has spoken to us by a Son, whom he appointed heir of all things" (Hebrews 1:1–2).

Christ's mind available, indeed infused into my thinking, feeling, and responding—awesome thought!

You may say, "That's too mystical for me. How does one manage that kind of trade—my mind for His? How does it actually play itself out in the life of one who seeks to be a true disciple—a lifelong Christ-follower?" Peter is a prime example of one committed to grow where and when he was planted, keeping his mind and heart open.

Peter and the Mind of Christ

Most growing Christians find it easier to identify with the apostle Peter than any other of Christ's inner circle. He was a good man whose exuberance often caused him to throw caution to the wind. All he needed from Jesus was a command, "Come," and he walked on water (Matthew 14:25–31). He loved Jesus passionately and was impulsive in his actions—a combination that was seen when he cut off the ear of a guard coming for Jesus (Matthew 26:51). Peter was quick to boast, once telling Jesus, " I will never desert you." His betrayal that very night brought him bitter tears of remorse (Matthew 26:33, 74–75).

But Peter could also speak courageously and with great wisdom. He was the first of all the apostles to identify Jesus as the Christ with this confession, "You are the Messiah, the Son of the living God." Jesus blessed Peter then and announced the establishment of His everlasting church.

The book of Acts, in reporting the early days of that church, gives Peter a prominent role. His powerful messages and works of healing the sick resulted in his imprisonment for some time. When he was released with orders not to teach in the name of Jesus, he encouraged the church to pray for even greater boldness (Acts 4).

As the church grew in numbers and identity, the most visible Christian leaders were persecuted. Severe reprisals caused many to flee for their lives, but the risen Jesus mustered this scattered church to bring even more into the fellowship. Peter found these displaced ones in their new homes and brought them encouragement and strength. He became an itinerant preacher, sharing from his experience and understanding, and he continued to perform miracles of healing. News of the resurrection of Dorcas, greatly loved member of the church in Joppa, spread quickly throughout the region, and many believed as a result (Acts 9:36–43).

Finally, no doubt out of sheer exhaustion, Peter decided to spend some time in Joppa on the Mediterranean Sea, with Simon the tanner. One afternoon, while waiting for lunch to be prepared, he went up to the rooftop to pray. That simple spot became as much a temple for Peter as the mountain of the burning bush was to Moses.

Tired and hungry, he was no match for the warm sun. When he drifted off in a trance, Peter saw a sheet filled with every kind of animal considered unclean by the Jews—snakes and vultures and worse. God's message to Peter was "Get up, Peter. Kill and eat." Peter answered what any faithful Jew would have been obliged to say. "By no means, Lord; for I have never eaten anything that is profane or unclean."

Expecting God's commendation, he was no doubt confused by what the messenger said instead: "What God has made clean, you must not consider unclean."

Three times that strange vision appeared. What was Peter to make of it? He had hardly begun to sort out all its implications when two slaves and a soldier called out for him. The fact they were Gentiles created somewhat of a problem; as Gentiles, they were unclean. Peter could not invite them in and certainly could not offer them food under Simon's roof. He and his host would become unclean and be required to go through a ritual cleansing ceremony—or would they? Already the new church was casting aside Hebraic laws not appropriate for these new Christ-followers. Did this rule qualify for revision as well? Still confused, Peter followed his heart, invited them in and gave them lodging.

Why had the men come? The centurion whom they represented, they said, had sent them in response to the message of an angel. They were, according to the angel's instructions, to accompany Peter to Caesarea so that they might hear what he had to say. Indeed, the centurion and his invited relatives and close friends were waiting to hear Peter's message.

Peter must have wondered if his vision on the rooftop could be connected some way with the purpose of these visiting Gentiles. It was not Peter's nature to turn down any opportunity to preach Christ, but he felt an even greater urgency to share his newest lesson from the rooftop experience. So the next day he, the men from Caesarea and several believers from Joppa set out.

Upon their arrival Peter began his message with, "I truly understand that God shows no partiality, but in every nation anyone who fears him and does what is right is acceptable to Him." With this the angels and the "great crowd of witnesses" must have roared, "Yes! He got it! Go Peter!" While Peter was teaching, the Holy Spirit fell on these Gentiles, and they began "speaking in tongues and extolling God" (Acts 10:46), to the astonishment of the Jewish Christians who had accompanied Peter from Joppa. The service closed with a joyful baptismal service.

What does one do when the rules suddenly change? Peter had been taught all his life that certain dietary laws, most of which related to meat, should be followed. These restrictions had served his forebears for generations, and were a test of Jewish orthodoxy. Now the vision on Simon's rooftop put all his prior beliefs to the test. Peter had to know God's intention. Were all the dietary laws upended? What of other Jewish laws and rules, thought to be sacred and enduring? Would they be repealed as well? Perhaps laws regarding certain people—lepers, menstruating women, eunuchs—needed reinterpretation.

Discovering the Mind of Christ

Peter was confused by the vision on Simon's roof. Just as he began to deal with his perplexity, the men sent by Cornelius appeared. But even this interruption seemed to be a part of the lesson God had for him. In Acts 10:9–48 we discover the steps he took to seek God's mind.

First, *he prayed.* In fact, he went to the roof of Simon's house with the expressed purpose to pray, and God honored his intention with a vision that would change him and enlarge the church's fellowship for time to come.

God often uses the time we have reserved for prayer as His time to give new insights, if we would only give Him time to speak to us. Instead we "say our prayers" and are on our way before God has a chance. "Stay a little longer," He seems to say. "I have so much I want to tell you." We zip in and out of prayer as though He were a casual acquaintance, not the declared Lord of our lives. If we would only listen in the silence until He speaks, we would learn of Him, grow to be more like Him.

We live in such a noisy age. Car salesmen shout their bargains on TV; you can hardly find an eating place with a friend for a quiet talk. Companies even purchase machines to create "white noise" to filter out extraneous noise in the workplace. Families buy sleep machines with the sounds of the surf, rain, and other supposedly restful sounds to hush the unrelenting barrage of noise that echoes the day's busy-ness. So accustomed are we to the cacophony of sound around us that we are uncomfortable with silence. "Be still, and know that I am God!" (Psalm 46:10). Be still and hear Him.

Secondly, Peter *reflected on prior learning.* As a little boy in the synagogue he heard his teachers stress the importance of a kosher diet, and as a result not one bite of pork or camel, nor any other meat forbidden by the Law, had crossed his lips. How did that prior learning match up with the vision on Simon's roof? Even though the Old Testament contains many references to the *missio dei* as God's offer of salvation to all nations, common Jewish understanding was that God only embraced the Jews.

Third, Peter *was open to the new lesson.* Throughout the night before they left for Cornelius' house, Peter no doubt lay awake trying to discern the lesson God was revealing. While walking the distance the next day, he surely prayed and listened for God's voice. His traveling companions' sense of urgency was contagious. God was preparing them all for something great. They must have felt it. Puzzled by the seemingly conflicting messages,

Peter continued to think and pray.

Upon their arrival at Cornelius's home, Peter found the expectant Cornelius with his relatives and close friends. Four days earlier, an angelic messenger had instructed Cornelius to go to Joppa to find a man called Peter. Now that all parties were gathered together in the presence of God, they awaited his message.

By this time Peter began to see the fuller implication of his vision. "What God has made clean, you must not call profane," had referred not only to animals but also to these Gentiles. In determining his words, *he relied on the Holy Spirit*. Peter had hardly started speaking when Cornelius and his friends began to speak in tongues and praise God. All the new Gentile converts were baptized on the spot. So hungry were they for further understanding that Peter remained with them for several days.

Peter had listened to the Spirit's challenge. At Cornelius's house, when the Holy Spirit fell upon those who heard Peter's message, the Christ-followers who had traveled with Peter from Joppa were astonished. "The gift of the Holy Spirit has been poured out on even the Gentiles!" Then it was clear that God's message of eternal salvation was for all humankind, all nations, all peoples. These were defining moments for the universal church. The promise, extended throughout time, that God loved *all* the world was being fulfilled. Peter preached the inclusive message of this truth, and today we join in the celebration.

"For there is no distinction between Jew and Greek; the same Lord is Lord of all and is generous to all who call on him. For, 'Everyone who calls on the name of the Lord shall be saved'" (Romans 10:12–13).

Peter, the strong leader, held great influence over the

early church leaders, and when he was called to Jerusalem to explain his actions, he told of his experience in Cornelius's home and declared, "If then God gave them the same gift that he gave us when we believed in the Lord Jesus Christ, who was I that I could hinder God?" (Acts 11:17). Because Peter was open to change, he powerfully persuaded others to do likewise.

We have to note also that Peter *acted on his partial understanding*. While he was still thinking on the vision and pondering the meaning, he went with Cornelius and his group because the Spirit told him to. He learned to put his full weight on the direction of the Spirit, which he had learned to trust. From that day forward, Peter worked diligently to share Christ with Jews and non-Jews, confident that the broadening of the kingdom had been God's plan from the beginning.

The World at Our Door

If Peter were in the US today he no doubt would be reminded of his experience at Pentecost. He would remember how tongues of fire accompanied the coming of the Holy Spirit, and how people, gathered in Jerusalem from faraway places, heard God's message in their own tongue.

In the twenty-first century "Parthians, Medes, Elamites, and residents of Mesopotamia, Judea and Cappadocia"—well, maybe not those specific people groups, but certainly from all points of the globe, have gathered in the US. Undoubtedly, Peter would plead with God for the ability to speak so that all would understand in their own language.

The world has literally come to our door. Students are arriving in record numbers, seeking a quality education. Tragically, some of these foreign students are never invited into our homes or our churches, and we miss the opportunity to give testimony of the Christian faith to them. Professionals from other countries are recruited for jobs in the US when adequate numbers of qualified workers here are not available. Others come here seeking asylum from repressive governments or greater opportunity for themselves and their children, becoming citizens of this country. It is not surprising that these new residents will develop places of worship in keeping with their own religion, many of which are strange to us—mosques, temples, shrines. Some Americans who have long been estranged from the church are fertile ground as proselytes to different beliefs and swell the ranks. Suddenly, we find that Islam is the fastest growing religion in America. How do we, evangelical Christians, respond? In hostile retorts, rejecting these "foreign" religions? By publicly targeting them for triumphalistic evangelical blitzing?

The religious pluralism in America is only one reason that we Christians must strive to be stronger, better-equipped disciples of Christ. Does Peter's experience in learning new truths provide a viable approach for us?

To Be A Lifelong Learner

1. *Pray for understanding and direction*. Claim Christ's promise in Matthew 21:22, "Whatever you ask for in prayer with faith, you will receive." Pray for your own understanding, for your dependence on the guidance of the Holy Spirit. Pray especially that God will show you His plan for your involvement in His work.

2. *Reflect on prior learning*. Read Scriptures such as Isaiah 56:6–7 that remind us that God will indeed accept anyone from anywhere who truly believes. Romans 11:13–18 was given to Gentiles, telling of their

being grafted into the Vine, assuring them of a place in the kingdom. Isaiah 60:1–3 concludes: "Nations shall come to your light, and kings to the brightness of your dawn." Matthew 28:19–20, charging us to go throughout the world teaching and baptizing "all nations," has been used in the past to mobilize Christians for worldwide missions. Today "going" may only require a trip to your office or to an ethnic restaurant or to get a manicure, but it still involves a measure of fear. God's Word has many references to fear. Verses such as 1 John 4:18 remind us that "perfect love casts out fear," and sends us to our prayer closets once again.

3. *Be open to the new lesson.* Following God is a dynamic experience. You may remember as a child going up to the baptistery after a service to inspect the "sins" that had been washed away. Surprise! They were invisible! Preschoolers often picture God as a kind of Santa Claus with a white robe. "When I was a child, I spoke like a child, I thought like a child, I reasoned like a child; when I became an adult, I put an end to childish ways" (1 Corinthians 13:11). As women, we are sometimes tempted to grab a "truth" from the past and hold tenaciously to it, refusing to consider an alternative view. But as lifelong learners we remain pliable to the Holy Spirit's shaping, willing to learn, open to change. He has so much to teach us, but only if we willingly submit to His instruction. The process of spiritual maturity is continual.

4. *Listen to the Holy Spirit's challenge.* Few inventions have made instant communication possible as has the cell phone. In a crowded department store or on the street, a ringing telephone causes men and women alike to reach for pocket or purse to retrieve the instrument that immediately puts them in touch. The Holy Spirit,

as near to us as life itself, awaits our call. The Spirit provides our immediate connection with the Almighty, and longs to instruct us, to inspire us, to challenge us. He sends nudges, impressions, and questions in order to give guidance and direction. Just as the Holy Spirit directed Peter in his journey of understanding new truth, so He will clarify any confusion in our minds if we listen and expect.

5. *Be open to change.* Every new endeavor requires risking of one kind or another. Making changes in our spiritual lives, however, demands unusual confidence and courage, qualities only bought with the currency of prayer and faith, especially when those required changes take us outside our level of comfort. What new truth does God want to teach you?

6. *Act on your partial understanding.* While still pondering the meaning of the vision, Peter followed the understanding he had. You may not know God's full plan in relating to the different religions in our midst, but knowing His desire to draw all the peoples of the world to Himself, we, the church, must do our part.

"I am learning from Jesus how to lead *my* life, my *whole* life, my real life," as Dallas Willard says. To understand what Jesus would do in my life will take much study of His life, much prayer, much help from the Holy Spirit, and a lifetime of learning. Let's get started!

CHAPTER 11

Ready for Anything

"Here I come, ready or not!" Many of you remember this warning from a game of "hide-and-seek" when we were children. The call meant that the prescribed count had been completed and the "hunted" should be ready. The seeking would begin.

Since those happy days the words "Here I come" can send chills up my spine. Are you ready for the final exam? To commit your life to this man? For the job interview? For the delivery room? To see your children grow up? To face retirement? For death?

Regardless of our age, we can expect many changes in our lives. For some changes we plan and work with purpose and joyful expectation. Others come like a bolt out of the blue and leave us frightened, perplexed and even devastated. And we hear the words again, "Are you ready? Here I come, ready or not."

In seeking indigenous music for a hymnbook to be used in Togo, missionary Patsy Eitelman had asked churches to submit recordings of their music. While evaluating the recording submitted by a Tem congregation she did a double-take. Although most of the words were unintelligible to her, one word came through with remarkable clarity, *ischokoto*, the word for underwear. Could her ears be deceiving her? She asked Toubaye', her associate, why the word underwear would be used in a Christian song.

Toubaye' laughed and said, "The refrain, 'hold up my underwear,' is an expression used by the old men. The song tells about the Day of Judgment."

"But what does holding on to your underwear have

to do with Judgment Day?" Patsy asked.

"In Togo a man strips down to his shorts or underwear when doing hard work or battle," he responded. "Sometimes they perspire and have difficulty keeping them from slipping down. So a 'hold up my underwear' day is an extremely demanding day when you don't know which way to turn."

Another expression like this might be more familiar to you—to "gird up your loins" in Bible times referred to tucking the loose ends of one's outer garment into the belt. Men girded up their loins for running (1 Kings 18:46), for battle (Isaiah 5:27), or for service for a master (Luke 12:35).

One such reference is Exodus 12:11, when God was telling the captive Israelites how to eat the Passover meal so that they would be ready to leave Egypt quickly: "This is how you shall eat it: your loins girded, your sandals on your feet, and your staff in your hand." They were to be ready for a long and difficult journey. God told Job many years later to gird up his loins like a man, for he would hear a mighty defense of Himself, and Job was to be ready.

Ready for World Events?

My husband Bill and our two little daughters arrived in Indonesia for the first time in June 1963. We knew the tenuous nature of the government, and had been told by one personnel director of the mission board that we could probably only expect to stay three or four years before the Communists overthrew the government. At the first meeting of our little cadre of missionaries in Bandung, Java, the discussion centered on evacuation plans. Four months pregnant, I had visions of trekking through the mountains and down to the capital city,

Jakarta, hoping to find a boat or plane to take us out. The doctor who was also in language school must have seen my expression of terror, for he said, "Don't worry, Dellanna, I'll keep my instruments sterile, and be ready for your delivery anytime, anywhere." It reminded me of the words Jesus spoke to the disciples about the peril of the end times: "Woe to those who are pregnant and to those who are nursing infants in those days! For at that time there will be great suffering . . . " (Matt. 24:19,21a)

The doctor's promise of help was good news. The bad news was the situation itself. But we were prepared.

Residents of the US sought to prepare themselves in 1962 when a military crisis suddenly emerged in Cuba. Soviet Premier Nikita Khrushchev, believing that future wars would involve strategic nuclear rockets, had created the USSR's Strategic Rocket Forces. Because of the expense of building intercontinental missiles, members of the Strategic Rocket Forces proposed using Cuba as a missile site, and in early 1962 began sending 22,000 Soviet soldiers and technicians to be prepared to launch medium and long-range ballistic missiles.

When President John Kennedy learned that a missile was actually on a launching site, he declared on October 22, 1962, that the island of Cuba was under quarantine. It was a preemptive strike intended to disarm the Soviet leaders. He also announced that U.S. forces would confiscate "offensive" weapons that might be found in the quarantined zone.

Our family was living in Fort Worth, Texas, where Bill was in graduate school. Our daughter, Denise, a second-grader, attended a public school nearby. For some time the school had held bomb drills—the children went into the hall, sat on the floor, and protected their heads with their arms. Knowing the peril our country faced, we were not totally surprised when Denise came home one day with a note alerting us to the school's plan in response to the impending disaster. She was to take to school a container of water and a limited amount of food, as well as a blanket. We had already followed directions printed in the newspaper in order to be prepared at home for possible disaster, such as storing up canned goods and non-perishable foodstuffs, water and other necessities. When we read the list of things Denise might need at school in case of an attack, frightening images of people running in hysteria came to mind. At times like this families became separated. We feared the agony of not being able to protect our own children!

Fortunately, as you know, Kennedy's threat had its hoped-for effect, and on October 28, Khrushchev announced that construction of the sites had been stopped. Denise brought her bottle of water and blanket home, and things returned to normal. Today, however, I cannot watch TV coverage of families running from disaster, panic and desperation registered on their faces, without thinking, "It could be us." And why not us?

Of all the nations of the world, the US is among the most blessed. Except for the American Revolution and the Civil War, no war has been waged on our soil. Before the infamous terrorist attacks on the World Trade Center and the Pentagon on September 11, 2001, and with the exception of the attack on Pearl Harbor, not even one battle had been fought in the US.

But since the September 11 attacks, the subject of readiness for *any* eventuality is on everyone's mind. Newspapers once again describe how to prepare for an attack, and families are instructed to create a disaster plan and practice carrying it out. Tips for recognizing suspicious letters or packages containing a hazardous material, what to do if evacuated, and how to escape a burning or collapsed building expand the newspaper columns. Even though we know that not every contingency can be anticipated, we can certainly take simple steps to ensure that our families and communities have the best chance to survive emergencies, whether they are brought about by nature, accident or terror attack.

The US is arguably the most powerful nation in the world. Each year people from many countries enter our borders seeking asylum and in search of "the American dream." We have lived in relative safety and generally enjoy adequate health care. Our constitution grants many freedoms, including the freedom of religion. We are truly blessed as a nation.

But our "blessedness" has been tested. Are prosperity and good fortune assured into the future? If not, are we ready to face adversity, prepared to be leaders under God's command in whatever circumstances?

Americans were caught up in a swell of patriotism immediately following the terrorists' first attacks. Our nation's flag graced our homes and businesses, and the pledge of allegiance to Old Glory carried new resolve. Compassion for the victims and their families stimulated gifts of multiple millions of dollars. Our churches were full. We held our children a little closer to us. All because we were not ready. We never fully acknowledged our vulnerability before.

Jerked into a new reality, our heightened fears escalated. Where would they attack next? Are we their target? Can we prevail against an ill-defined enemy? Who are they anyway? Why do they hate us so much? We attempt to muffle the sound of our own questioning fears by staying informed, involving ourselves in meeting emergency needs, and pleading for God's intervention. We pray for courage and deepen our commitment to spiritual preparedness. With all of today's fears and uncertainty, how can Christian women be prepared for any eventuality?

Ready to Manage Ourselves

During World War II the American populace, citizens of all ages, committed to self-imposed austerity for the sake of the war effort. Shoes, gasoline, tires, and sugar were among the items rationed. We placed decals on the windshields of our cars asking the question, "Is this trip really necessary?"

Even children had a part. Every week we bought savings stamps and placed them in special books. When a book was filled, we exchanged it for a war bond. We participated in scrap metal drives for the war effort. Paper goods were at a premium, and cooking oil and chocolate seldom appeared on the grocer's shelf. For the sake of the necessities of the war, we willingly endured a season of sacrifice.

Since those years, we Americans have become soft. With no need to deprive ourselves of anything, we have become both wasteful and careless. We are annoyed when the price of gasoline rises. We are inconvenienced by escalating home heating costs. Once again we are reminded that our appetites for "gas-guzzling" cars and our demand for energy have contributed to the depletion of natural resources. Rather than curb our insatiable taste for luxury and "the good life," we whine for more access. We send out a cry for new sources of fuel with little concern for the safety of the environment and the possible exhaustion of future resources.

We want whatever it takes to live in the style to which we have become accustomed.

And we use water, life-sustaining water, as if there were an endless supply. A recent study reports that 31 countries currently face water shortages. By the year 2025, 2.8 billion people—35 percent of the world's projected total population of 8 billion people—will face water shortages. The report cites as causes increased industrial development, increased reliance on irrigated agriculture, massive urbanization, and rising living standards.

In the 20th century while the world population has tripled, water withdrawals increased **by over six times**. The study concludes with the prediction that in the twenty-first century more and more countries will experience water crises and even risk outright conflict over access to scarce freshwater supplies. They urge that finding solutions should become a high priority now.

Are we truly ready to become responsible world citizens and caring Christian sisters and brothers?

Ready or Not
America's governmental leaders struggle along with the heads of other nations to find safeguards for the protection of the natural resources we hold in common. But as Christians we cannot back away from our own responsibility for fairly utilizing the gifts God has provided the world. We are increasingly, and effectively, involved in disaster relief, but are we equally willing to guard our use of water, oil, and monetary wealth? What is our part in deeds that endanger humankind?

The parable of the talents begins, "For it is as if a man, going on a journey, summoned his slaves and entrusted his property to them" (Matthew 25:14).

Sound familiar? God has entrusted unbelievable assets to us. Let's gird up our loins, Christian women, put on our sweats, and get ready for our job as managers of the universe.

As stewards of God's creation, we must **be informed** of the conditions in which we live, both here and internationally. News media keep us knowledgeable regarding current needs locally and around the world. As information becomes available, **pray** for those involved—victims, relief workers, and families of those in crisis and emergency and intermediate caregivers. Pray for yourself. Pray about what part beyond prayer that you might feel led to take.

Awareness should result in personal conservation of natural resources and concern for the needs and safety of others. **Be involved** in areas of need. In every disaster there are needs for gathering resources (clothes, money, volunteers), forming prayer support groups, lobbying for appropriate legislation, caring for children so others can act and so much more. Pray for courage to take the necessary steps. Deepen your commitment to spiritual preparedness.

"Finally, be strong in the Lord and in the strength of His power. Put on the whole armor of God, so that you may be able to stand against the wiles of the devil. Therefore, take up the whole armor of God, so that you may be able to withstand on that evil day, and having done everything, to stand firm" (Philippians 6:10–11,13).

Watch and Wait
"Keep awake, therefore, for you do not know on what day your Lord is coming. But understand this: if the owner of the house had known in what part of the night

the thief was coming, he would have stayed awake and would not have let his house be broken into."
—Matthew 24:42

Too bad the five foolish virgins in the story that follows this passage didn't follow this principle. You remember they were distinguished from the five wise virgins by one thing: they were not ready. They had lamps, but they did not have a reserve of oil.

In those days the custom called for a groom to claim his bride at her house and bring her to his own home. Friends patiently awaited their arrival, after which the celebration would begin. Since no one knew the exact arrival time, the anticipation would build up in the waiting crowd. The bridegroom, hoping to intensify the excitement, would arrive in the middle of the night in the hope he would catch them napping. Sure enough, the story goes, every one had given up hope that the bridal couple would come on this night and settled down to sleep.

Suddenly, the cry went up, "Look! Here is the bridegroom! Come out to meet him!" The ten maidens got up quickly and began to trim their wicks. The foolish virgins were in trouble. Their lamps had run out of oil. When they begged the five wise virgins to share their oil, they were told there was not enough for them all. "You'd better go to a shop and buy some for yourselves." While they were gone, the bridegroom closed the door and the foolish young women were left outside.

If this were *just* a story, we would say, "Too bad." But the parable has a deeper meaning: being prepared for the return of our Lord. How important it is to be constantly in a state of readiness for his coming!

Jesus underscored the significance of being ready:

"Be dressed for action (gird up your loins) and have your lamps lit; be like those who are waiting for their master to return from the wedding banquet, so that they may open the door for him as soon as he comes and knocks. Blessed are those slaves whom the master finds alert when he comes" (Luke 12: 35–37a).

Whether girding up our loins, filling our lamps, or holding up our underwear, constant readiness for events of eternal significance secures the blessings of our Father.

Watch and Work

Imagine yourself as one of the ten virgins waiting for the bridegroom. It may be hard to sit around watching and waiting for someone to come. If that's all we had to do, surely we could remember to buy an extra bottle of oil. But with the busy-ness of our lives, the important matters often fall prey to the immediate—the tyranny of the urgent. The speed of our lives whips us around like a pinwheel in a hurricane. Our schedules are so convoluted that we can scarcely remember the last time that our "to do" list had every item checked off.

Our lives are characterized by a fast pace—too often a pace without focus. Each morning we begin frantically running off to work or a meeting, getting the children to school on time, shopping for groceries, and on and on. We push every hour to see if we can get just one more thing in before bedtime. Guilt plagues us when we don't have time to visit our neighbors or see a friend in the hospital. We all claim the poster that says, "The faster I run, the behinder I get."

Fast change keeps us constantly off balance. In 1970, Alvin Toffler described a new disease called "future shock." This condition, he claimed, was the result of "too much change in too short a time." More than twenty-five years later, Stephen Bertman wrote in his book *Hyperculture: The Human Cost of Speed*, "the pace of social change has increased even more." According to his assessment, because of the fast pace of change, we have forgotten the past and have no vision of the future. Technology allows us artificial power that reduces the physical effort necessary to accomplish a task. It also shortens the time necessary for its completion. As a result we are faced with new opportunities, new processes, and new tools. Keeping up in any given field calls for on-going training and equipping. Technology was supposed to bring us more leisure time but instead we are busier than before.

The need to make fast decisions forces us into poor choices. We rush into a deal without full understanding because we fear that we might miss out on something. Advertisements in local newspapers announce rare sales, offering convenient times of business and easy payoff schedules. "Last chance, reduced prices never before seen!" they cry. TV ads and online marketing make purchases easy and attractive. Before we know it, charge cards are filled to the max, and still we have the insatiable urge to purchase more and more.

Our time, too, is quickly consumed in activities that are good, but have little or nothing to do with God's kingdom. What will it take to come to grips with our addiction to spending of time, money, and influence? How can we turn our focus back to His tasks? How can we ready ourselves to be the wise stewards that God has ordained us to be when all around us the world squeezes us into its mold?

Ready, Set, Go

Believe it or not, establishing priorities in life is not a new problem. The Bible speaks of the choices believers must make in order to be in a constant state of readiness. Let's look at some of them.

1. **Lay aside.** The Scriptures tell us we should lay aside those things that would become a hindrance. "Therefore, since we are surrounded by so great a cloud of witnesses, let us *lay aside* every weight and the sin that clings so closely . . . " (Hebrews 12:1).

I've never been a competitive runner and never will be. But if I did, I'd take my cues from the professionals. They know that any extra weight can slow them down. An overweight sprinter has no hope of defeating a lithe, disciplined runner. No serious competitor would select heavy, cumbersome clothing and expect to cut time off her record. Obviously, in spiritual matters, to be ready for whatever comes our way, we must be diligent in sloughing off the weightiest matters—chief of which is sin. As God forgives us for our sins, the Holy Spirit enables us to resist the temptation that comes to each of us.

"*Therefore, rid yourselves* of all sordidness and rank growth of wickedness, and welcome with meekness the implanted word that has the power to save your souls" (James 1:21). In the day in which we live it is difficult to impossible to avoid the smut that swirls around us. Television, movies, books—even everyday conversation—are host to bad language and bad morals. We hear foul language so frequently it soon becomes innocuous. If we aren't careful, it even slips out of our own mouths. Those who then hear our witness have difficulty in reconciling the two messages. If we are to be ready for God's service, we must lay aside all that opposes God's word planted in our hearts.

"*Rid yourselves,* therefore, of all malice, and all guile, insincerity, envy and all slander." Or as The Message puts it, "So clean house! Make a clean sweep of malice and pretense, envy and hurtful talk" (1 Peter 2:1). Even seemingly small matters loom large when a witness is at stake. The state of the heart is everything. Words and deeds issue out of the heart and betray harbored prejudices and distrust. No wonder the Spirit reminds us to take inventory and to do away with all that is malicious and hurtful.

2. **Travel light.** When Jesus sent out twelve disciples on a preaching mission, he said, "*Take nothing* for your journey, no staff, nor bag, nor bread, nor money—not even an extra tunic" (Luke 9:3). Luke does not report any comments resulting from this command, but can't you imagine our responses? "What! No purse? No food or money? How do you expect us to live?" And that was precisely the point Jesus made when he issued the order. They would have to depend entirely upon God to provide all they needed.

We occasionally read of individuals who are left in the inner city as an experiment with little or no money to fend for themselves for several days or weeks. When the time is complete, they understand better what it means to be resourceful in the midst of poverty. Most of us shy away from anything so risky. Instead we try to anticipate needs and shore up our reserves.

If God called you to pull up stakes and move to another part of the world to accomplish a purpose, how long would it take for you to get ready? Are your belongings so many that prompt obedience would be difficult? Are your credit cards the "master of charges?" Right now this author is feeling very uncomfortable. It is so easy to get burdened down with "things." What would it take for us to travel light?

3. **Establish priorities.** "I do not consider that I have made it on my own: but *this one thing I do*" (Philippians 3:13a). A vision statement guides a company or organization in setting priorities for its work. Paul clearly knew the parameters of his ministry, "the heavenly call of God in Christ Jesus." Developing a vision statement requires a frank assessment of values, assets, goals, and purposes of the company (or individual.) If you began your vision statement with Paul's own words, how would you flesh it out? What are your abilities, your spiritual gifts, your goals? The spiritual exercise of creating a personal vision statement equips a Christian to be ready for use by God.

4. **Manage time.** "We must work the works of him who sent me while it is day; night is coming when no one can work" (John 9:4). Remember those foolish virgins? They forgot the work of the day (getting extra oil), so when night came, it was too late. Thankfully, if you have experienced new birth in Christ, you haven't missed the bridegroom's wedding. But if we fail to make proper use of the daylight hours, we may miss blessings that God intends for us to enjoy, or opportunities for spontaneous service.

Open your calendar for this month. Look at the day with the most marks. (If you don't record your activities, try it. It tells us much about ourselves.) Now, just imagine that God has a special assignment for you that day. Could you squeeze it in? We keep ourselves so booked up that we have little flextime.

We plan good things—lots of good things—and too often neglect the better things. "I just don't have time to be a good neighbor. The children's schedules are so crazy that I just can't visit folks in the hospital. I wanted to teach in Vacation Bible School, but that was the exact week I had to drive my son to baseball camp each day. I'd love to attend Bible study but, I don't know, something always comes up. I meant to talk with my congressperson about debt relief, but I just don't know how." At the end of life, will we look back over the years and wish we had spent our time differently? Time is precious, so we need to invest it in eternal matters.

5. **Manage money.** "No slave can serve two masters; for a slave will either hate the one and love the other, or be devoted to one and despise the other. *You cannot serve God and wealth*" (Luke 16:13).

During one of Jesus' messages, a man shouted out to him, "Teacher, tell my brother to divide the family inheritance with me." Jesus replied that he had no intention of arbitrating their differences, but he warned: "Take care! Be on your guard against all kinds of greed; for one's life does not consist in the abundance of possessions." (Luke 12:15.) If any one verse needs to be emblazoned on Christian hearts it is this one. We may be scrupulously careful about how we earn our money and even faithfully give our tithe to the church but still miss the heart of this command.

Jesus then told a parable about a successful farmer. So bountiful were his crops that storage was a huge problem. Congratulating himself for his success, the farmer planned on living many years in luxury. But that night he died. Poor man! He never had the opportunity to enjoy the abundance he had accumulated.

Jesus closed his story with this caution: "So it is with those who store up treasures for themselves but are not rich toward God." Riches in themselves are not evil. Paul told young Timothy that God gives us all things for our enjoyment. But he advised him to warn the wealthy about being haughty or setting their hopes on the uncertainty of riches. They are to do good, to be rich in good works, generous, and ready to share, "thus storing up for themselves the treasure of a good foundation for the future, so that they may take hold of the life that really is life" (1 Timothy 6: 17–19).

Money can provide for our needs and even our enjoyment. But it can also be a trap, snatching away the best that Jesus has to offer His faithful followers. It is our choice. Are you ready?

Ready—For Anything

Is it possible, really, to be prepared for anything and everything? Since we cannot see into the future, can we devise a plan for all eventualities?

During Y2K, people around the world feared what might happen during the changeover from 1999 to 2000. Many older computer systems, in order to conserve space, used only the last two digits of a year. Therefore when the year 2000 rolled around, it would appear as 1900, causing some computers to lock up or give faulty information. Because of the wide use of computers in industries, all sorts of dire predictions were made. Electric and telecommunications companies, banks, and other businesses spent multiple millions of dollars making corrections in their computer systems. They made assurances to their customers, who found little comfort in them. People bought canned food and water, built underground shelters and prepared for—whatever. And when the clock registered 12:01 A.M., January 1, 2000, the expected cataclysmic disaster failed to occur. The stash of non-perishable food, flashlights and other items lasted well over a year. Today we laugh about the Y2K fears.

But not all crises are resolved so happily. The terrorism we face today is real. Its intent has been demonstrated. We watch the storm clouds gather with fear and anxiety. Can it be, however, that God has allowed this evil that His power might be more clearly seen? Is this the impetus for revival in our nation? Are we ready to be God's instruments?

In the midst of this present reality Satan works in the personal realm as well. Somewhere a teenaged son, with every promise for a successful future, will put the barrel of a gun in his mouth and pull the trigger. The president of a large business will learn that an employee he thought was faithful has embezzled millions. A child will receive an adult's life sentence for murdering fellow students at school. How can we ever be ready for such catastrophes?

The fact of the matter is that when these present crises are resolved, we can be sure that others will take their place. A greeting card reads, "This is not a test. If it had been a test, we would have been given better instructions." True, crises do not arrive with easy-to-follow directions for disassembling. But those of us who know Christ can move boldly and confidently into the unknown. In the strength of our Lord we find adequate wisdom and strength in these evil days. "Finally, be strong in the Lord and in the strength of his power. Therefore, take up the whole armor of God, **so that you may be able to withstand on that evil day, and having**

done everything, to stand firm" (Ephesians 6: 10,13). When we have done all we can, God provides what we lack. So get ready for whatever with confidence. He is the great enabler, our shield and our buckler.

CHAPTER 12

Doing Everything in Love

And can it be that I should gain
An interest in the Savior's blood?
Died He for me, who caused His pain?
For me, who Him to death pursued?
Amazing love! How can it be
That Thou, my God, should die for me?
—Charles Wesley

Have you ever gone to the Bible to seek support for a retaliatory action you are considering? On our worst days we think that perhaps we can find permission for kicking an offender in the shins—at least figuratively. We like the verse in Proverbs commanding that we heap coals of fire on the heads of our enemies (Proverbs 25:21–22). However, that seemingly drastic measure does not give us permission for revenge, according to Bible commentaries. Rather than being punitive, they report, the phrase instead means to be a comfort to your enemy. Although the meaning of this expression is obscure, the intent is clarified in Jesus' teaching in the Sermon on the Mount: "Love your enemies and pray for those who persecute you" (Matthew 5:44). His actions, especially on the Cross when He prayed for the forgiveness of His adversaries, provided undeniable evidence of returning good for evil.

Some years ago a group took the opportunity to publicly criticize decisions my organization had made. Since the "coals of fire" strategy was not appropriate, I needed an alternative plan. The ideas in 1 Corinthians 16:13 seemed to contain the direction I needed to take: "Keep alert, stand firm in your faith, be courageous, be strong."

Aha! That was it! I needed to stand ready to deflect any further attack and be bold and gutsy. If they struck again, I would be prepared. Then my eyes fell on the verse following: "Let all that you do be done in love."

Love. I had to admit that my planned response had little to do with love. And yet the two verses in tandem form a powerful response to anyone like me seeking guidance. Faith, courage, strength—and love. Only three chapters earlier, Paul in his letter to the church in Corinth had placed love in another list, along with faith and hope. Again, love surpasses them all.

Love. Of course, we all know its importance in the Christian life. The Bible speaks often of love. But for Christian women of our day the call to love has never been more urgent. Babies die for the lack of a loving touch. Drunks huddle in dark alleys, numb with loneliness and hopelessness. Our sisters paint happy faces on lost souls, without dignity and without love. Churches wither and die on the vine when love does not pervade the life of the body.

Throughout the chapters in this book we have been confronted with evidence that we sail in a sea of change—sometimes dark and foreboding, and other times bright and filled with promise. Love holds the key to the ultimate outcome. Finding the source of all love, we turn to God, who is love.

Love Is Costly
You cannot speed-read through the book of Hosea. Just as you get the cruise control set, you read the words the

Lord spoke through/to the prophet and all momentum comes to a screeching halt: "Go, and take for yourself a wife of whoredom and have children of whoredom" (Hosea 1:2).

We know immediately that this book is different from most. Reading on we learn that Hosea did indeed marry Gomer, a harlot, who bore him a son. In the remaining chapters we read of Gomer's betrayal of her marriage vows. After having two more children, she fled, abandoning her husband and children for the life of a prostitute. The names of the offspring foretell the dissolution of the marriage.

Jezreel: God sows.

Lo-ruhamah: not pitied. Possibly fathered by someone else.

Lo-ammi: for he was "not my people"—not Hosea's.

Gomer chose to desert the husband who loved her and children who needed her, all for the life of a harlot. Food and clothes and strong drink, poor substitutes for the sacrificial love Hosea offered, finally brought her to ruin. She was put up for sale on the slave block. And Hosea *buys her back*, for 15 shekels of silver, a homer of barley, and a measure of wine.

By this point in the story the reader is well aware of the power of the allegory. In order for Hosea (and ultimately those of us who have read his book) to begin to comprehend the love of God, he first must experience the rejection of a treasured love. The Israelites, in spiritual harlotry, had departed from God's teachings and chased after pagan festivals and new moons. Throughout the book the God-figure Hosea reaches out to his heart-love, and feels pain at her betrayals.

Were it not for this captivating story, it would be difficult for us to fathom the great anguish of God when we forsake Him. Like Gomer, we have left all that is pure, perfect, and righteous to pursue our own lusts. In our natural state we hardly ever give a thought to God's agony. When we finally are spent and our alternatives vanish, God loves us still. His love is wondrous, holy, and scarcely understandable to finite minds.

In Love, God Seeks

A friend says, " My husband chased me so long I finally caught him!" In every spiritual love affair, however, God is without question the initiator. He is proactive, one who seeks and woos the objects of His love. "We love, because He first loved us." The burning question throughout all time is *why*? What commended us to God? His love can never be contingent upon our worth. Imagine Gomer on the auction block, a slave to her last paramour. Dirty, her hair tangled from days of neglect, all pride of life gone. She was hardly worth the ransom Hosea paid for her. Her flagrant betrayal of Hosea should have killed any affection he had for her long before. But his heart remained open to her. He continued to be steadfast and faithful to his commitment to her.

In June of 2000, a small group of women gathered in a prominent US city for a prayerwalk. Their intended destination was a several-block area of sin industries—gay bars, exotic dancers, stores for sex objects, and prostitutes. The prayerwalkers carried gifts in their hands to give to the women they met inside their businesses. As they encountered the women, they introduced themselves, and said, "I have gifts for you." Then they gave them a Sacagawea gold dollar and a Bible. "You are worth more to God than gold. This is His book of love." Could they believe it? Other well-meaning Christians had probably delivered a different evaluation of the women's place in God's kingdom. Some of the women had perhaps been relegated to never-never land, never to be chosen, never to be worthy, never to be loved. Now another assessment has been received, one of hope and expectation.

We should now stop and take inventory. Ever worshipped an idol? No. Ever been employed as an exotic dancer? Oh, no. Been a prostitute? Heavens, no! But wait a minute. Lest we begin to feel pious and commendable, let us remember who we are. And who God is. Not a one of us could garner enough worth to justify God's love of us. Yet He has loved us since before we were born.

God's Love Is Persistent

When Gerald Ray, minister of music at Houston's First Baptist Church, and his wife, Trevalynn, came to Indonesia to lead a music conference, they left their little daughters at home. As they told them goodbye, Trevalynn said, "Now girls, remember your manners." One looked a bit anxious, and then blurted out, "Could you tell them to us again?"

As Jesus neared the Cross, did he have questions concerning the time when He would no longer be physically present with His followers? Had he covered all pertinent and necessary information? Did they fully understand? Would they remember?

Jesus had little time for review. Thankfully, the Holy Spirit would provide needed reinforcement. Jesus had told them, "I still have many things to say to you, but you cannot bear them now. When the Spirit of truth comes he will guide you into all truth" (John 16:12–13). But one important fact was clear in His departure from this world. Nothing would ever change His love for them. "Having loved his own who were in the world, he loved them to the end" (John 13:1). He loved His followers, including us, with an everlasting love.

When Indonesian MK Jerry Buckner was a little boy, his mother, Mary Ann, called him. "Jerry, we got a letter from Grandmother," she reported. "She said to tell you she loves you."

"I know it," he responded.

"You know it? How do you know it?" his mother asked.

"I just *feel* it all the time."

Do you feel God's love all the time? Remember, God never changes. He is the same yesterday, today, and tomorrow. If we feel an estrangement, a distancing in our relationship with Him, it is not He who has moved. Rather our disobedience and spiritual lethargy pull us away from His tender care and everlasting love. Just as the father of the prodigal son anxiously awaited his return, so God yearns for ours.

Jesus' thoughts were for us to the end. In His last spoken prayer with the apostles He prayed, "I made your name known to them, and I will make it known, so that the love with which you have loved me may be in them, and I in them" (John 17:26). God's love, distilled in Christ's willing sacrifice, never fails.

God's Love Redeems

Hosea trudged with heavy feet and heavy heart to the market. He dreaded seeing her; his friends had reported her appearance. Not a pretty sight. Yet he longed to see her, longed to hold her in his arms. "I will now allure her, and bring her [home], and speak tenderly to her," he thought. "There she shall respond as in the days of her youth" (Hosea 2:14,15).

Soon this would all be over. After he paid her price, she would be his again. He checked the cart that carried the barley, the price of her redemption. A few coins and bottle of wine he carried in his bag would provide enough to complete the sale.

The sale. He stifled a guttural laugh. Paying for that which is already yours. Strange. Soon she would be twice his. He hurried his pace, not wanting to delay another minute in seeing her—in making her his own again.

How God loved Israel! As hard-hearted and hard-headed as they were, God persisted in loving them and giving them second and third chances. His love extends to all generations. Now our generation is on the slave block. Without Christ's offer of redemption we have no way out. The Ephesians, like all generations before and since them, had a chance to receive Christ's offer. "In him we have redemption through his blood, the forgiveness of our trespasses, according to the riches of his grace that he lavished on us" (Ephesians 1:7–8). God's redemption, freely given, was bought with a great price.

"No one has greater love than this, to lay down one's life for one's friends," Jesus told His disciples. "You are my friends if you do what I command you. I do not call you servants any longer, because the servant does not know what the master is doing; but I have called you friends, because I have made known to you everything that I have heard from my Father. You did not choose me but I chose you . . . I am giving you these commands so that you may love one another" (John 15:13–17).

God proved His love "in that while we were still sinners Christ died for us." We cannot learn all there is to know about love in a lifetime, but to know God is to yearn to be more like Him. The Bible gives us in words the teachings He demonstrated while here. The answers to the hurts inflicted by others? Love. To misunderstandings? Love. To disagreements? Love. Do everything in love.

Thou Shalt Love Thy God

The belief in a divine presence has been part of humankind since the beginning of time. People around the world tend to seek a connection to this deity in various ways. Animism, which centers its quest among nature and all its objects, still exists in many parts of the world. Although the majority of the people living in Indonesia consider themselves Muslims, the practice of animism still pervades everyday life.

While we were living in Indonesia, a committee came to my husband, Bill, with a strange request. The owners of an outdoor market planned to enlarge their area in order to accommodate the needs of a growing population. As they had proceeded with their plans, they ran into a serious problem. The preparation of the land required cutting down a large tree believed to house a god to whom people brought prayers and gifts each day. The builders recognized that to destroy the tree, and the god it reportedly contained, would incite riots among the people in the community. The answer then was to exorcise the god, and Bill was requested to be the exorcist. (No seminary course had ever provided him an order of worship for such a ceremony!) The practice of animism, in which many gods are believed to inhabit rocks, trees and other objects, is based on fear and appeasement.

While animism requires its adherents to keep many

deities happy, Islam has a very strict code of conduct, the first of which is to give evidence of belief in the one God, whose name is Allah, and Mohammed as his prophet. Islam, meaning "submission," calls for its followers to be faithful in four additional matters: obedience to five ritual daily prayers, the annual fasting period, giving alms to the poor, and a once-in-a-lifetime pilgrimage to Mecca. Obedience to these requirements balanced against their sins determines their entrance into heaven.

Other peoples believe that suffering for wrongdoings can earn forgiveness. The predominant religion in the Philippines is Catholicism. Although the Catholic Church claims no attachment to it, a group bent on purging their sins by physical suffering centers its activities near their churches. On Good Friday hundreds participate in "The Rite of the Flagelantes." We witnessed it for ourselves in 1964. Each year hundreds of men who feel their sins have been unusually grievous strip their upper bodies of clothing and don hoods, covering their faces. Then they beat themselves with whips that have broken glass and other sharp objects attached to the ends. As the whip bites into the skin, the blood begins to flow. Some enter bodies of saltwater at the end of the day. Some, it is said, actually are crucified on crosses, reenacting the sufferings of Jesus. If only they knew that Christ has already paid the supreme sacrifice for our sins; only confession is necessary for our forgiveness.

Judaism requires obedience to the Hebraic law. Those laws are contained in the Torah and have served to direct the lives of faithful adherents. Non-compliance requires appropriate sacrifices or offerings.

Only Christianity offers redemption by grace of a

loving Savior. A benevolent God who loves His people and works for their good is unheard of in any other belief system. How blessed we are to be adopted by our holy God! Drawn by His love, He invites us to live courageously, confidently, and peacefully in Him.

A Matter of Love

Contemporary women changed by God's love find reason and strength to follow His example. Without the power of the Spirit, genuine, unconditional love would be as impossible as it was in the first century. Yet we are urged to make love the guiding principle in our lives. In fact, when Jesus was asked which commandment was the greatest, He responded, "'You shall love the Lord your God with all your heart, and with all your soul, and with all your mind.' This is the greatest and first commandment. And a second is like it: 'You shall love your neighbor as yourself'" (Matthew 22:37–39).

Christianity stands alone in offering a love relationship between God and the penitent. He sets standards for our lives, but obedience is based on the trust in a loving Father and a desire to obey and serve Him. Our motivation—not fear, but love—is derived from a desire to please and imitate our Father.

When we pull away from His embrace and seek our own way, God waits for our return. Like the father of the prodigal son, He accepts our acts of repentance. When we neglect to communicate with Him, He waits for our return. When, like children, we become petulant over perceived slights, He seeks our trust.

But true love endures. God never changes, He never moves. He is the constant in our lives. The One who first loved us, loves us to the end.

Look once again at Proverbs 31, at our virtuous lady.

Nowhere in the passage do we see the word *love*. But is there evidence of a loving life? A trusting husband receives her good care. She sacrifices sleep in order to provide a healthy meal for her children. She's generous to the poor, opening her hand to the needy. She seems to demonstrate the elements of a loving Christian life.

Christian woman in the twenty-first century, could it be said of you, "She does everything in love"? If love is so important that Jesus lifted it above all the other commandments, surely we should be willing to ask ourselves, "Do I do everything in love?"

The Bible's "love chapter," 1 Corinthians 13, offers us the best descriptors of love. The first three verses tell us what love is *not*: eloquent speech, loud noise, prophetic power, wisdom or intellect, earth-shaking faith, generosity, or courage. Verses 4 through 8 tell us what love is. The following is the translation found in *The Message*:

> *Love never gives up.*
> *Love cares more for others than for self.*
> *Love doesn't want what it doesn't have.*
> *Love doesn't strut,*
> *Doesn't have a swelled head,*
> *Isn't always "me first,"*
> *Doesn't fly off the handle,*
> *Doesn't keep score of the sins of others,*
> *Doesn't revel when others grovel,*
> *Takes pleasure in the flowering of truth,*
> *Puts up with anything,*
> *Trusts God always,*
> *Always looks for the best,*
> *Never looks back,*
> *But keeps going to the end.*

What a good checklist for the virtuous woman of today! Try reading the list again, keeping in mind a certain person or group—your husband, children, a friend, an enemy, your boss, a neighbor—those with whom you have regular contact. Do you consistently demonstrate loving qualities in every relationship? Love does not exist in a vacuum but always in association with another.

Paul Chose Phoebe

Paul was careful to underscore this principle as he established churches throughout his missionary journeys. Even after he departed from an area, he continued to pray for the young churches and wrote letters to reinforce his teachings. As extensive as Paul's travels were, he longed to go to Rome where he could both encourage the church and be encouraged by them. Finally, he made arrangements to go to Spain, stopping by Rome on the way. In order for the Roman church to know of his coming, and hopefully to receive some financial help for his journey, he wrote them a letter. Most biblical scholars believe Paul was in Corinth when the letter was penned. The epistle to the Romans has been determined to be the most significant theological treatise ever written.

Who then should carry this important letter to the Roman church? The courier must be a mature believer, one who was competent to share in the spirit and truth of its contents. Obviously, the person must be physically able to make the difficult trip and financially equipped to cover the costs. Paul chose a deacon of the church in Cenchrea, the seaport of Corinth. He chose Phoebe, because she satisfied all the criteria. In addition, she had been a benefactor to many, including Paul himself. The hard, rugged trip took her through areas previously evangelized by Paul. We can imagine that she took opportunity to stop by each church to greet them and hear their news.

As Phoebe read the passages from the letter she carried to the Roman church, she must have felt the Lord's presence. She could almost hear Paul's own voice: "Let love be genuine; hate what is evil, hold fast to what is good; love one another with mutual affection; outdo one another in showing honor" (Romans 12:9–10).

Her heart resonated with Paul's words in identifying love as the mark of a true Christian. How she must have longed for love to be a hallmark of her own church in Corinth! Instead the members were forming rival, competing units. "I belong to Paul," some said. Others were proud to acknowledge Apollos or Peter as their leaders. So much divisiveness!

What about the church of the twenty-first century? Already divided into denominations, we further split off as fundamentalists, moderates, liberals, Calvinists. We line up behind political parties and argue about what kind of music we should sing in church. The world reads the newspaper articles about our most recent battle and wonders how we can make the claims of Christianity. They don't care a whit about our sectarian battles. They want to see Jesus.

We need a Paul to stand before us and say to us the words he wrote to Phoebe's church: "Now I appeal to you, brothers and sisters, by the name of our Lord Jesus Christ, that all of you be in agreement and that there be no divisions among you, but that you be united in the same mind and the same purpose" (1 Corinthians 1:10).

Love, A Timeless Virtue

Loving somebody is so easy, if we can choose the some-body. We love our husbands even when they fuss about the burnt toast. Our grandchildren are cute even in their antics. After all, they're only children. Friends are excused from a slight because we understand all they're going through. Loving the ones we—well, we *love*—is not the problem. Since Jesus placed love above every other virtue, it is necessary to go beyond what is natural or spontaneous, to deal with the more intentional facets of love.

Paul was careful to warn believers of the dangers in not loving. To the Galatians he wrote: "If . . . you bite and devour one another, take care that you are not consumed by one another" (Galatians 5:15).

Hatred causes blindness. This makes sense, does it not? When a woman has hatred in her heart she is unable to interpret a situation correctly. Anger and hostility result in poor judgment and bad decisions. Like a cancer, it consumes time and energy. It grows if not contained, and ultimately results in death. When such a condition finds its way into the church, it feeds on itself, it divides, and if not squelched can ultimately destroy the fellowship.

The church in Corinth was torn by factions on multiple issues. In assimilating the Greeks into the fellowship, the matter of eating meat offered to idols often came up. While some of the church members claimed freedom from the old Jewish laws, others believed that meat offered to idols was tainted and should not be eaten. Paul wrote to the church at Corinth, "Knowledge puffs up, but love builds up." Rather than becoming a stumbling block to the weak members, Paul said, "I will never eat meat, so that I might not cause one of them to fall" (1 Corinthians 8:13).

Paul would lead us to believe that we should be more concerned about building a fellowship of love in the church than building a block to "get my agenda approved."

Our personal part is to "outdo one another in showing honor" (Romans 12:10).

"The greatest of these is love"—love of spouse, children, friend, foe, the poor. Everyone. Lavishly, without hope of gain, not being puffed-up.

A three-year-old was on the heels of his mother wherever she went. If she stopped to do something and then turned around, she would trip over him. She gave him several toys, hoping to interest him, but he just smiled and said, "I'd rather be here with you."

As she turned away, he was right behind her, taking her every step. Finally, after stepping on his toes the fifth time, she asked in exasperation, "Why are you doing this? Why are you acting this way?"

With bright eyes and sweet smile, he said, "Well, Mommy, my Sunday School teacher told me to walk in Jesus' footsteps. But I can't see him, so I'm walking in yours."

Someone learning to love as Jesus did seeks an earthly model. She watches you and follows your example. You may never notice her; but she sees your every smile, hears every word. Maybe someday she will have occasion to say, "When I grow up, I want to be just like you. You do everything in love."